A Gift from

Koren Publishers
Jerusalem

For more information
please contact

Bezalel Jacobowitz

bezalel@korenpub.com
www.korenpub.com
203 830 8509

MAGGID

Rogov's Guide to Kosher Wines
2010

Daniel Rogov

ROGOV'S GUIDE TO KOSHER WINES

2010

The World's 500 Best Kosher Wines

The Toby Press

Rogov's Guide to Kosher Wines 2010
First Edition
The Toby Press LLC

POB 8531, New Milford, CT 06776-8531, USA
& POB 2455, London W1A 5WY, England
& POB 4044, Jerusalem 91040, Israel

www.tobypress.com

ISBN 978 1 59264 261 8, *hardcover*

A CIP catalogue record for this title is
available from the British Library.

Typeset in Chaparral Pro by KPS

Printed in Israel

Table of Contents

Foreword

There can be no question but that kosher wines are on the way up in the world. The days when "kosher" meant primarily sweet red wines that were consumed primarily for sacramental purposes are long gone. More than that, the best producers of wines that are kosher have become and continue to be acknowledged as serious competitors on the market, their wines receiving increasingly favorable reviews from individual critics and from the most prestigious wine publications. High quality kosher wines are being produced in the USA, Israel, France, Italy, Germany, Austria, Hungary, Spain, Portugal, New Zealand, Australia, Chile and Argentina. In each of those countries the construction of state-of-the-art wineries, the ongoing cultivation of noble grape varieties, the use of more fully modern methods in the vineyards and the enthusiasm and knowledge of well-trained winemakers continue to yield an abundance of quality wines that compete comfortably with many of the fine wines of the New and Old Worlds.

Reflecting the enormous advances in the quality of kosher wines, many observant Jews who once perceived wine primarily as a beverage with which to celebrate various ceremonial events have come to discover that wine, when consumed in moderation, is an integral part of a cultured way of life. Equally important, with the realization that there need be no contradiction whatsoever between wine that is kosher and wine that is excellent, kosher wines are also making an inroad into the non-Jewish markets of the world.

The purpose of this book is to provide readers with an intimate knowledge of the five hundred best kosher wines that I have tasted or re-tasted during the last year. In that, the book is also meant to serve as a convenient guide for selecting, purchasing and storing wines, and deciding when to consume them. The introduction provides a brief social and historical background, as well as an overview of what makes wine kosher, while the major part of the guide is devoted to the wines themselves, offering tasting notes and scores for wines that are now on the shelves or are scheduled to appear within the next six to nine months. This also acts as a guide to wines that may still be stored in the cellars or wine refrigerators of wine lovers. The afterword provides an overview of how I do my own wine tastings, information for hosting a wine tasting party and a glossary of wine terminology.

How to Use the Guide

Wineries are arranged in the book first in order of their countries and then, within each country, in alphabetical order. In some cases, because wineries may be known under one name in Israel and another in the USA or UK, readers will find the alternative names listed in the index.

In cases where wineries release more than one series, the top-level series is presented first in the listings and each of the listings is arrayed from red to white wines. Where appropriate, the tasting notes are also divided into grape varieties such as Cabernet Sauvignon, Merlot, Chardonnay, etc. Each variety is arranged according to vintage year, from the most current releases to more mature wines that meet the qualifications for entry into the book, and each review concludes with a score and a suggested drinking window. A separate section is devoted to rosé, dessert and sparkling wines.

In some cases specific wines are represented in the book by more than one vintage year: When each of these vintage years passes the entry level for admission into the book and there is a good chance that these wines are still available in wine shops or in storage in people's homes.

Because Israel produces far more kosher wine than any other country, it is only reasonable to expect that many of the very best wines will be from there. The prerequisite for entry into this book (that a wine be of very good to outstanding quality) does not allow for all good kosher wines to be reviewed. Those seeking tasting notes for other Israeli or worldwide wines and for older vintages not represented can send an email to *rogovkosherbook@gmail.com* . All emails will be answered and notes on the wines in question be given for those wines I have tasted. It should also be noted that not all Israeli wines are kosher. To read about those wines one might consider purchasing the latest edition of *Rogov's Guide to Israeli Wines*.

One word of friendly warning to those who observe the laws of kashrut. All wineries in Israel and in the USA that produce kosher wines produce *only* kosher wines, but in France, Italy, Spain and other European countries, as well as in South America, many wineries produce both kosher and non-kosher editions of the same wine. It thus falls on the kashrut-observant to check each bottle to see that the appropriate kashrut certification is present.

Key to Symbols and Scores

THE WINERIES

In the case of American and Israeli wineries that produce a major series of kosher wines, each winery is rated as follows. Other wineries are not so rated because they produce only one or two kosher wines and even though their wines may be excellent, they are not always produced on an annual basis.

    ✶✶✶✶✶   A WORLD-CLASS WINERY, REGULARLY PRO-
                 DUCING EXCELLENT WINES

      ✶✶✶✶   CONSISTENTLY PRODUCING HIGH-QUALITY
                 WINES

        ✶✶✶   SOLID AND RELIABLE PRODUCER WITH AT
                 LEAST SOME GOOD WINES

SCORES FOR INDIVIDUAL WINES

   96–100   Truly great wines
    90–95   Exceptional in every way
    85–89   Very good to excellent and highly recommended
    80–84   Recommended but without enthusiasm

Note: Because this book deals with the best wines currently available, no wines scoring less than 85 points are reviewed.

DRINKING WINDOWS

A drinking window is the suggested period during which the wine is at its very best. The notation "best 2012–2015," for example, indicates that the wine needs further cellaring before it comes to its peak and will then cellar comfortably through 2015. "Drink now–2012" indicates that although the wine is drinking well now it will continue to cellar nicely until 2012. "Drink now" indicates that the wine is drinking well now but can be held for another year or so. "Drink up" suggests that the wine is at or past its peak and should not be cellared any longer. "Drink from release" refers to wines that are not yet on the market but are scheduled to appear within the next six to nine months.

As to Kashrut Certificates

The wines reviewed in this book have all received a kashrut certificate from a recognized rabbinic authority.

Introduction

Questions of Kashrut

Jews probably have the oldest codified relationship of any people to wine and until the period of the Roman occupation there was a thriving wine industry in the Holy Land. In fact, Israeli wines were so highly prized during those days that they were shipped not only to nobles in Rome, but to Roman outposts throughout Europe and North Africa. Then, two thousand years ago, after the onset of the Diaspora, when Jews were scattered throughout the world, winemaking became an extremely difficult proposition. In many places Jews settled in countries where the soil and climatic conditions were hostile to grape growing. More than that, even in lands where grapes could be grown, Jews were often forbidden to own land and therefore had none on which they might raise grapes.

Despite that, because wine was required for sacramental purposes, winemakers used whatever tools were at hand to make kosher wines, in many cases using table grapes and in others even using dried raisins. And, because a steady supply of fine grapes was unavailable, it became virtually impossible to produce high quality kosher wines. By the time Jews began to settle in America, the tradition of winemaking could begin once again, but at that time the Concord grape had come into favor and, if the truth be told, wines made from these grapes had a coarse, foxy character and were made sweet in order to make them more palatable. Over time, it was such sweet, coarse wines that came to be associated with kosher wine. For many years, wines that were kosher lacked sophistication and had a justifiably bad name. Even throughout much of modern-day Europe the situation was similar, the observant among the population who did seek kosher wines being for the most part unaware that the wines they received were very poor cousins to the best wines being produced. The truth is that those wines were not so much consumed by knowledgeable wine lovers as they were used for sacramental purposes. Such wines are still made, but are today perceived largely as oddities, consumed more out of a sense of tradition when performing kiddush and similar rituals. In nearly every country with a Jewish population, some continue to drink wine entirely for sacramental purposes. An increasing number have realized that any kosher wine is appropriate for such purposes, but others hold to the perceived tradition that such wines should be red, thick and sweet. Although such wines hold no interest for sophisticated wine drinkers, several large wineries continue to produce kiddush wines and there are wineries that focus entirely on these consumers. However, with kosher wines now being made from the most noble grape varieties in state-of-the-art wineries by talented winemakers, there need be no contradiction whatsoever between the laws of kashrut and the production of fine wine.

What Makes a Wine Kosher?

There are several major differences between the requirements for a wine to be kosher within Israel, and outside Israel. In order for an Israeli wine to be certified as kosher, several requirements must be met. As can easily be seen, none of these requirements has a negative impact on the quality of the wine being produced and several are widely acknowledged to be sound agricultural practices even by producers of non-kosher wines. Within Israel seven rules must be strictly followed:

1. According to the practice known as *orla*, the grapes of new vines cannot be used for winemaking until the fourth year after planting.
2. No other fruits or vegetables may be grown in between the rows of vines (*kalai hakerem*).
3. After the first harvest, the fields must lie during the sabbatical year, which follows a seven-year cycle. Each of these sabbatical years is known as a *shnat shmita*.
4. From the onset of the harvest only kosher tools and storage facilities may be used in the winemaking

process, and all of the winemaking equipment must be cleaned to be certain that no foreign objects remain in the equipment or vats.

5. From the moment the grapes reach the winery, only Sabbath-observant Jews are allowed to come in contact with them. Because many of the winemakers in the country are not Sabbath observant, this means that they cannot personally handle the equipment or the wine as it is being made and are assisted in several of their more technical tasks by Orthodox assistants and kashrut supervisors (*mashgichim*).

6. All of the materials (e.g., yeasts) used in the production and clarification of the wines must be certified as kosher.

7. A symbolic amount of wine, representing the tithe (*truma vema'aser*) once paid to the Temple in Jerusalem, must be poured away from the tanks or barrels in which the wine is being made.

Those producing kosher wine outside of Israel must follow only the fourth, fifth and sixth of these rules.

The Question of Wines That Are Mevushal

Some observant Jews demand that their wines be pasteurized (*mevushal*), especially in restaurants and at catered events, where there is the possibility that a non-Jew may handle the wine. This tradition dates to ancient times, when wine was used by pagans for idolatrous worship: the Israelites used to boil their wines, thus changing the chemical composition of the wine so that it was considered unfit for pagan worship. Wines that are *mevushal* have the advantage that they can be opened and poured by non-Jews or Jews who are not Sabbath observant.

Today, *mevushal* wines are no longer boiled. After the grapes are crushed, the common practice is to rapidly raise the temperature of the liquids to 176–194 degrees Fahrenheit (80–90 Celsius) in special flash pasteurizing units, hold it there for under a minute and then return the temperature, equally rapidly, to 60 degrees Fahrenheit (15 Celsius). There is no question that modern technology has reduced the impact of these processes on the quality of the wine, but most winemakers and consumers still agree that, with very few exceptions, wines that have been pasteurized lose many of their essential essences, are often incapable of developing in the bottle and quite often impart a "cooked" sensation to the nose and palate.

Some wines are produced in both regular and *mevushal* versions, the *mevushal* editions destined largely for the market in the United States and the United Kingdom as well as for the highly observant within Israel. Because it is almost impossible for anyone outside of the wineries to keep track of and taste all of these wines, no attempt is made within this book to report on such "double bottlings." Although a great many kosher wines destined to be served in restaurants or at public events continue to be produced using this technology, a glance at the international wine scene indicates that an increasing number of wineries are no longer using the pasteurization process in the production of their better wines. Although many *mevushal* wines will drink nicely for six months to a year after bottling, nearly all will show signs of deterioration after that. The truth of the matter is that only a few producers in the world, most notably those of the California wineries Hagafen and Herzog, have produced *mevushal* wines that are the equivalent in quality and perhaps even aging potential of their non-*mevushal* brothers and sisters. In Israel, none of the better kosher wines fall into this category.

Simply stated, a wine that is *mevushal* is no more or less kosher than a wine that is not. Those who are concerned with such issues will find the information they require on either the front or rear labels of all kosher wines, together with the notice of the rabbinical authority that granted the kashrut certificate.

Some Israeli Wines Are Kosher, Others Are Not

A great many people are surprised to learn that not all of the wines produced in Israel are kosher. A look at the current Israeli wine scene tells us that the wines of every large winery and the majority of medium-sized wineries in Israel are indeed kosher, but those of the smaller wineries are often not.

For many years, all of the wines produced in Israel were kosher, with the exception of those made in Christian monasteries. The reasons for this were and still are twofold. The first reason relates to the fact that a large proportion of the Israeli population, even among the non-religious, consumes only foods and beverages that are kosher. The second also has a clear economic basis—because only kosher products can be sold in most of the large supermarket chains in the country. Because the majority of wines produced in the country continue to be purchased in supermarkets, no large winery can afford to give up that considerable sales potential. In addition, kashrut is maintained because many of the wineries continue to target their export sales largely towards Jewish consumers worldwide.

The wines of several of the medium-sized producers and many of the boutique wineries have a somewhat different goal in mind—that of producing upper-end wines that are targeted towards higher-end and not necessarily kashrut-observant wine consumers both in Israel and abroad. The production of kosher wines, which demands additional staff (such as rabbinic supervisors), as well as fees to the rabbinic authorities, can add prohibitively to the costs and the eventual retail price of wines, which is especially onerous for small wineries.

Grape Varieties Used for Kosher Wines

The last two decades have seen a major change in the choice of grapes used to make kosher wines. Prior to 1985, as mentioned previously the vast majority of kosher wines in the United States were made from Concord grapes, which produced red wines that tended to be quite sweet and had an unpleasant musky aroma and flavor. The simple truth is that while Concord grapes are just fine for making jam, they are not capable of producing fine wine. In Israel, where wineries focused on light, white, and often sweet wine, the grapes planted were largely inferior clones of Carignan, Petite Sirah and Grenache for red and rosé wines, and Semillon, Emerald Riesling and Colombard for whites, those producing massive crops, the grapes not at all ideal for the making of fine wine.

It took several adventurous souls to change this. In Israel, a revolutionary tide swept the wine industry in 1983 with the opening of the Golan Heights Winery, and in the United States the change started with one large and one small winery—Herzog and Hagafen respectively. Those wineries forever changed world opinion about the potential of kosher wines.

Within Israel, the scene shifted dramatically with the development of vineyards planted with noble varieties, first on the Golan Heights, then in the Upper Galilee. Today, from the Negev Desert to the northernmost parts of the country, the focus is on many of those varieties that have proven themselves throughout the world. In the United States, a quantum change came about when the kosher wine scene moved from New York State to California, where soil and climate conditions as well as fine grape varieties were available. For the first time in hundreds if not thousands of years, kosher wines were produced that could stand comfortably alongside many of the best non-kosher wines of the world. The trend continued in Europe where many highly reputable wineries began to produce kosher editions of their wines for local consumption, as well as for export to North America, the United Kingdom and even Israel.

The grapes described in the following paragraphs are those most likely to be encountered today in kosher wines.

Red Wine Grapes

BARBERA: From Italy's Piedmont region, this grape has the potential for producing wines that, although light and fruity, are capable of great charm.

CABERNET FRANC: Less intense and softer than Cabernet Sauvignon, most often destined to be blended with Merlot and Cabernet Sauvignon, but even on its own capable of producing dramatically good, leafy, fruity and aromatic reds.

CABERNET SAUVIGNON: The most noble variety of Bordeaux, capable of producing superb wines. Often blended with smaller amounts of Merlot and Cabernet Franc. The best wines from this grape are rich in color and tannins, and have complex aromas and depth of flavors, those often typified by blackcurrants, spices and cedarwood. At their best, intriguing and complex wines that profit from cellaring.

CARIGNAN: An old-timer on the kosher scene, for many years this originally Spanish grape produced largely dull and charmless wines. In recent years, however, several wineries have demonstrated that old-vine Carignan grapes, especially those from fields that have been unwatered for many years, can produce interesting and high quality wines.

GAMAY: The well-known grape of France's Beaujolais region, this fairly recent introduction to the kosher wine scene is capable of producing light- to medium-bodied wines of fragrance and charm, intended primarily for drinking in their youth.

GRENACHE: Although this grape has traditionally done well in France's Rhone Valley and Spain, for many years it did not yield sophisticated kosher wines, most being somewhat pale, overripe and sweet in nature. Today, however, there is a growing move to cut back on the yield of the grape, the result being sometimes concentrated and intense wines of long cellaring potential.

MALBEC: Well known in France's Bordeaux, the Loire and Cahors, and the specialty grape of Argentina, this grape is capable of producing dense, rich, tannic and spicy wines that are remarkably dark in color.

MERLOT: Softer, more supple and often less tannic than Cabernet Sauvignon—with which it is often blended—but capable of producing voluptuous, opulent, plummy wines of great interest. A grape that has proven popular on its own, as it produces wines that are often easier to drink and are approachable earlier than wines made from Cabernet Sauvignon.

NEBBIOLO: The grape from which the Barolo and Barbaresco wines of Italy's Piedmont region are made. Still experimental in Israel and California but with the potential for producing perfumed, fruity and intense wines that are full-bodied and high in tannins, acidity and color, and have the potential for long-term cellaring.

PETIT VERDOT: Planted only in small quantities and used as it is in Bordeaux, primarily for blending with other noble varieties to add acidity and balance. Capable when ripe of producing a long-lived and tannic wine on its own.

PETITE SIRAH: Even though related only peripherally to the great Syrah grape, this grape is, at its best, capable of producing dark, tannic and well-balanced wines of great appeal and sophistication. For many years Petite Sirah was used too often to produce mass-market wines that tended to be hot, tannic and without charm. The potential of this grape is now being demonstrated well both in California and in Israel and an increasing number of truly excellent wines are appearing.

PINOT NOIR: Responsible for making the great red wines of Burgundy, Pinot Noir is a rising star on the kosher wine market. At its best the grape is capable of producing smooth, rich and intricate wines of exquisite qualities, with flavors of cherries, wild berries and violets, which as they age take on aromas and flavors of chocolate and game meat. In addition, Pinot Noir is used in Israel and California, as it is in the Champagne region of France, to blend with Chardonnay to make sparkling wines.

PINOTAGE: A South African cross between Pinot Noir and Cinsault, capable of being flavorful and powerful yet soft and full, with a pleasing sweet finish and a lightly spicy overlay.

SANGIOVESE: Italy's most frequently planted variety, found in the simplest Chianti and most complex Brunello di Montalcino wines, this is another grape recently introduced to the kosher world and is showing fine results, with wines that are lively, fruity and full of charm.

SYRAH: Some believe that this grape originated in ancient Persia and was brought to France by the Romans, while others speculate that it is indigenous to France. Syrah found its first glory in France's northern Rhone Valley, and then in Australia (where it is known as Shiraz). Capable of producing deep royal purple tannic wines that are full-bodied enough to be thought of as dense and powerful, but with excellent balance and complex aromas and flavors of plums, berries, currants, black pepper and chocolate. First kosher results from this grape have been exciting.

TEMPRANILLO: The staple grape of Spain's Rioja area, with recent plantings in Israel, this is a grape with the potential for producing long-lived complex and sophisticated wines typified by aromas and flavors of black fruits, leather, tobacco and spices.

ZINFANDEL: Although Zinfandel (the Italian variety of which is known as Primitivo) is an old staple in California, it is relatively new in Israel. Until recently the kosher wines produced were largely charmless semi-dry blush wines, those often referred to as "White Zin." Recently planted high-quality vines from California and in Israel offer the potential for producing full-bodied to massive wines, moderately to highly alcoholic, with generous tannins and the kind of warm berry flavors that typify these wines at their best.

White Wine Grapes

CHARDONNAY: The grape that produces the great dry white wines of Burgundy and is indispensable to the production of Champagne. The most popular white wine grape in the world today, producing wines that can be oaked or un-oaked, and range in flavor from flinty-minerals to citrus, pineapple, tropical fruits and grapefruit, and in texture from minerally-crisp to creamy.

CHENIN BLANC: Originating in France's central Loire Valley, a grape capable of producing long-lived wines with honeyed notes. Until recently used in Israel to produce ordinary, semi-dry wines but now being shown by several small wineries to produce exciting dry and sweet wines.

GEWURZTRAMINER: This grape originated in Germany, came to its glory in Alsace and has now been transplanted to many parts of the world. Capable of producing aromatic dry and sweet wines that are often typified by their softness and spiciness, as well as distinctive aromas and flavors of litchis and rose petals.

MUSCAT: There are many varieties of Muscat, the three most often used being Muscat of Alexandria, Muscat Canelli and Black Muscat, each of which is capable of producing wines that range from the dry to the sweet and are almost always typified by their perfumed aromas.

RIESLING: Sometimes known in Israel as Johannisberg Riesling, sometimes as White Riesling and sometimes simply as Riesling, this noble German variety has the potential to produce wines that, although light in body and low in alcohol, are highly flavored and capable of long aging. Typified by aromas and flavors of flowers, minerals and lime, and when aged, sometimes taking on a tempting petrol-like aroma. This grape should not be confused with Emerald Riesling, which is a cross between the Muscadelle and Riesling grapes developed in California primarily for growth in warm climates, and which produces mostly semi-dry wines of little interest to sophisticated wine consumers.

SAUVIGNON BLANC: At its best in the Loire Valley and Bordeaux for producing dry white wines, this grape is capable of producing refreshing, sophisticated and distinctively aromatic and grassy wines, often best consumed in their youth.

SEMILLON: Although this native French grape was used for many years in Israel and South Africa to produce largely uninteresting semi-dry white wines, its susceptibility to noble rot is now being used to advantage to produce sweet dessert wines with the distinctive bouquet and flavors of melon, fig and citrus. Several small wineries have recently begun producing interesting dry whites from this grape.

TRAMINETTE: A not overly exciting hybrid, a derivative of the Gewurztraminer grape, developed primarily for use in cold-weather New York State and Canadian climates.

VIOGNIER: This grape produces the fascinating Condrieu wines of France's Rhone Valley. Capable of producing aromatic but crisply dry whites and full-bodied whites, some of which have long aging potential.

Worldwide Kosher Vintage Reports: 2000–2008

The first formal vintage tables appeared in the 1820s and since then wine lovers have relied on them to help make their buying and drinking decisions. As popular as they are, however, it is important to remember that because all vintage tables involve generalizations, there are no firm facts to be found in them. In a sense, these charts are meant to give an overall picture and perhaps to supply clues about which wines to consider buying or drinking. In making one's decisions it is wise to remember that the quality of wines of any vintage year and in any region can vary enormously between wineries. Also worth keeping in mind is that vintage reports and tables such as those that follow are based on what most people consider "quality wines" and not those made for everyday drinking, which are not intended for aging. More than this, estimates of drinkability are based on wines that have been shipped and stored under ideal conditions. Equally important, whether one enjoys drinking wines in their youth, their adolescence, their early adulthood or their maturity is very much a matter of personal taste.

Following are short reports on the last five vintage years. Vintage years are rated on a scale of 20–100 and these numerical values can be interpreted as follows:

100 = Extraordinary
90 = Exceptional
80 = Excellent
70 = Very Good
60 = Good but Not Exciting

50	= Average but with Many Faulted Wines
40	= Mediocre/Not Recommended
30	= Poor/Not Recommended
20	= Truly Bad/Not Recommended
NYT	= Not Yet Tasted

The Kosher Vintage Chart ⊠

	Israel	California	France Bordeaux	France Burgundy	Italy Piedmont	Italy Tuscany	Spain
2008	89	NYT	NYT	NYT	NYT	NYT	89
2007	86	90	86	88	NYT	86	86
2006	87	86	87	87	92	93	86
2005	89	90	94	92	92	91	90
2004	88	87	86	87	92	93	92
2003	89	90	90	88	86	90	86
2002	82	90	86	90	77	83	79
2001	90	91	90	86	91	91	85
2000	89	89	93	85	95	90	83

⊠ The vintage year generalizations above are entirely for kosher wines and do not necessarily represent the quality of the overall harvest for non-kosher wines in each region.

Drinking Habits

Within the "Jewish World"

Nearly all of the better wine stores of the major cities of North America, the United Kingdom and France have at least a small section devoted to kosher wines, and in recent years the wines of Israel have taken a more prominent space on those shelves alongside kosher wines from California, France, Spain, Australia, Chile and Argentina. The reception of kosher wines is gradually getting warmer, such wines now being reviewed more regularly and more favorably in magazines devoted to wine as well as in the weekly wine columns of many critics. Such wines are also appearing on the menus of an increasing number of prestigious restaurants, some of those restaurants kosher, others not.

More important, in the last five years it has become increasingly apparent that those who keep kosher have begun to acquire a greater appreciation for wine as something not only used in religious rituals but as an integral part of a cultured lifestyle. Wine consumed in moderation is increasingly perceived as one of the ideal beverages with which to accompany meals, especially meals taken with other people, and a good deal of research shows that few who consume primarily kosher wines drink alone or without food. Other research shows that amongst Jews, wine is not often associated with drunkenness, and certainly not associated with increased automobile accidents.

Wine consumption in the United States and Canada among those who observe kashrut now parallels that of the average American—that is to say, a consumption of some 9–11 liters of wine annually, which is considered moderate consumption by nearly all studies in the fields of medicine and epidemiology. Consumption of kosher wines in the UK among those who keep kosher is just a tad higher, some 10–11 liters annually.

Within Israel

From the founding of the state in 1948 until 1997, annual Israeli wine consumption held steady at about 3.9 liters per capita. Although there is some debate about precisely how much wine is being consumed by Israelis currently, recent years have seen a major increase, and consumption now stands at 6–7 liters annually. This figure puts Israelis far behind the French and Italians, who consume 56 and 49 liters respectively, or even the Australians, who consume 20 liters per year.

The increase in consumption reflects of course the increasing quality of kosher wines. It also reflects the fact that more and more people, observant or not, are traveling abroad and dining in fine restaurants, where wine is an integral part of the meal, and so are learning to order wine to accompany their meals. Today, many are also touring the fine wineries of Bordeaux, Tuscany and the Napa Valley.

In addition to showing a growing appreciation of wine in general, those who consume kosher wines are moving in several directions that can be seen among the general population as well. Consumption is shifting from semi-dry to dry wines, from whites to reds, from light to heavier wines and most importantly, there is a movement towards buying higher-quality wines. Twenty-five years ago, more than ninety percent of the kosher wines produced in the world were sweet. Today, nearly eighty percent of the wines produced are dry.

THE WINES AND THE WINERIES: DRY RED AND WHITE WINES

Dry Red and White Wines

CYPRUS

LAMBOURI, YA'IN KAFRISIN, LIMASSOL, CYPRUS, 2007: Dark garnet with orange and purple reflections, a blend of Cabernet Sauvignon, Mavro and Grenache Noir grapes showing medium- to full-bodied, with soft, gently caressing tannins and good balancing acidity. Opens to show an appealing range of blackcurrant, blackberry and purple plum fruits, and notes of bitter orange peel, those on a background of white pepper and Oriental spices, with the tannins and fruits rising on the finish. A fine first kosher wine from a boutique winery. Drink now–2011. Score 89.

FRANCE

Bordeaux

CHÂTEAU COURTIEU, BORDEAUX, 2007: Garnet towards royal purple, medium-bodied, with soft tannins and gentle spicy wood, opens to reveal a basic berry-black cherry personality and, on the moderate finish, a hint of white chocolate. An appealing entry-level wine. Drink now–2011. Score 86.

CHÂTEAU D'ARSAC, MARGAUX, 2003: Ruby towards garnet in color, medium-bodied, with soft tannins and showing a simple but pleasing enough berry-cherry personality and a near-sweet white chocolate finish. Drink now. Score 86.

CHÂTEAU CHEVAL BRUN, ST. EMILION, 2002: Deep garnet in color, this full-bodied blend of Merlot, Cabernet Sauvignon and Cabernet Franc (75%, 15% and 10% respectively), shows chewy tannins in good balance with spicy wood and an appealing array of berry, currant and earthy-herbal aromas and flavors. Drink now. Score 88.

CHÂTEAU COUTET, DEMOISELLES DE COUTET, BORDEAUX, 2004: Ruby towards garnet in color, medium-bodied, with fruit-forward berry, black cherry and purple plums supported by hints of earthy minerals. Tannins and fruits rise on the finish. Drink now–2011. Score 86.

BARONS EDMOND & BENJAMIN DE ROTHSCHILD, HAUT MÉDOC, 2005: When tasting this wine blind, I was ready to take an oath that it was the 2001 wine that I was sampling, so similar are the two. As was that earlier release, medium- to full-bodied, with chunky tannins giving the wine a Provençal note but opening nicely to reveal black fruits on a background of minerals and white pepper. Drink now–2012. Score 88.

BARONS EDMOND & BENJAMIN DE ROTHSCHILD, HAUT MÉDOC, 2004: Deep garnet, medium-bodied, with firm tannins that seem not to want to settle in and integrate but opening to reveal blackberry, currant, Oriental spices and, on the medium-long finish, a hint of mint. Drink now. Score 87.

BARONS EDMOND & BENJAMIN DE ROTHSCHILD, HAUT MÉDOC, 2003: An oak-aged blend of 60% Cabernet Sauvignon and 40% Merlot. Medium- to full-bodied, dark ruby towards garnet in color, with soft tannins and gentle wood integrating nicely to show a generous array of currant, red and black berry fruits, all on an appealingly spicy background. Drink now–2013. Score 90.

CHÂTEAU FROMBAGUE, ST. EMILION, 2001: Dark ruby towards garnet, medium- to full-bodied, with soft tannins and gentle sweet cedarwood influences coming together nicely with blackberry and currant fruits, those matched nicely by hints of minted chocolate. Well balanced and moderately long with tannins rising comfortably on the finish. Drink now. Score 89.

CHÂTEAU GISCOURS, MARGAUX, 2005: Well done. Garnet towards royal purple with orange reflections, full-bodied, with soft tannins integrating nicely. Opens on the palate to show red and black berries, cherries and notes of citrus peel. Long, mouth-filling and generous. Best from 2011. Score 90.

CHÂTEAU GISCOURS, MARGAUX, 2004: Dark garnet, full-bodied, with gripping tannins and rather generous sweet cedar notes, those opening slowly in the glass to reveal black fruits and hints of mocha. Drink now–2014, perhaps longer. Score 90.

CHÂTEAU GISCOURS, MARGAUX, 2003: Garnet towards royal purple, medium- to full-bodied, with soft tannins and hints of spicy wood integrating nicely to show black cherry, blackberry and vanilla notes. On the long finish a generous hint of olives and Mediterranean herbs. Drink now–2013. Score 89.

CHÂTEAU GISCOURS, MARGAUX, 2001: Dark garnet, with orange and purple reflections, medium- to full-bodied, with soft, well-integrated tannins and an appealing array of blackberry, currant and earthy-mineral aromas and flavors. Drink now. Score 90.

CHÂTEAU GRAND PRINCE, ROBERTO COHEN SELECTION, BORDEAUX 2005: Medium-bodied, garnet towards royal purple in color, with soft tannins and notes of near-sweet cedarwood. A fruit-forward wine with blackberries, currants and purple plums, those with hints of Oriental spices. Moderately long. Drink now. Score 89.

CHÂTEAU LABÉGORCE, MARGAUX, 2004: Think of this as the younger brother of the non-kosher edition if you will—younger, ready to drink earlier, but reflecting much the same personality. Medium- to full-bodied, with firm tannins only now starting to recede and opening in the glass to reveal blackberry, raspberry, black cherry and white chocolate, all leading to an appealing After-Eight minty note. A generous wine, but not one for long term cellaring. Drink now–2012. Score 89.

CHÂTEAU LABÉGORCE, MARGAUX, 2003: Well done. Dark garnet towards royal purple, medium- to full-bodied with silky smooth tannins and spicy wood integrating nicely and opening on the palate to reveal currant, blackberry and black cherry fruits, those supported nicely by earthy minerals and a hint of spiciness. Moderately long. Drink now–2011, perhaps longer. Score 89.

CHÂTEAU LABÉGORCE ZEDE, MARGAUX, 2003: Medium- to full-bodied, with generous but gently mouth-coating tannins and showing fine balance between those, wood and fruits. A blend this year of Cabernet

Sauvignon, Merlot, Cabernet Franc and Petit Verdot (50%, 35%, 10% and 5% respectively), showing blackberry, currant and blueberry notes, those supported nicely by hints of spices and Mediterranean herbs. Long and generous. Drink now–2012, perhaps longer. Score 90.

CHÂTEAU LABÉGORCE ZEDE, MARGAUX, 2001: Full-bodied, with fine balance between gently mouth-coating tannins and dusty oak. Opens to reveal a complex array of blackcurrant, blackberry and purple plum on a spicy and vanilla-rich background. Generous and long and perhaps finally showing its best. Drink now–2011. Score 90.

CHÂTEAU LABÉGORCE ZEDE, BARRAIL DE ZEDE, BORDEAUX SUPERIEUR, 2001: A blend of Merlot, Cabernet Sauvignon and Petit Verdot (60%, 30% and 10% respectively). Ruby towards garnet in color, medium-bodied with soft, almost unfelt tannins and appealing berry, black cherry and currant fruits on a lightly spicy background. Lacks complexity but a good bet with food. Drink now. Score 86.

CHÂTEAU LA CLARE, CRU BOURGEOIS, MÉDOC, 2005: Dark royal purple in color, medium- to full-bodied with gripping tannins and generous oak that need time to settle down. Opens to reveal flavors and aromas of blackberries, cherries and cassis fruits, those on a background of roasted herbs. Moderately long. Best 2011–2014. Score 88.

CHÂTEAU LA CLARE, MÉDOC, 2003: Dark garnet towards purple, a traditional Bordeaux blend (Merlot, Cabernet Sauvignon, Cabernet Franc and Petit Verdot) with firm tannins and toasty oak now integrating nicely. On the nose and palate blackberry, black cherry and purple plum fruits, those matched by earthy minerals. Mouth-filling and moderately long. Drink now–2012. Score 88.

LA DEMOISELLE D'HAUT-PEYRAT, HAUT-MÉDOC, 2003: The second wine of Château Peyrat-Fourthon but with no need at all to feel second-class. Garnet towards royal purple, a blend of Cabernet Sauvignon, Merlot, Cabernet Franc and Petit Verdot (55%,36%, 5% and 4%

respectively), almost but not quite a twin to the first wine (described on p.24), this one showing medium- to full-bodied, with good balance between soft tannins, wood, acidity and fruits. Opens with blueberries and blackberries, goes on to show blackcurrants and chocolate, and on the medium-long finish, a hint of espresso coffee. Drink now. Score 88.

CHÂTEAU LAFON-ROCHET, ST. ESTÈPHE, 2003: Dark garnet towards royal purple, medium- to full-bodied, with soft tannins integrating nicely, a well-rounded and well-balanced wine with blackcurrants, wild berries and generous vanilla and toasty oak. Drink now–2011. Score 88.

CHÂTEAU LA FRANCE, MÉDOC, 2000: Deep garnet in color, a medium- to full-bodied blend of Merlot, Cabernet Sauvignon and Cabernet Franc (70%, 15% and 15% respectively). Aged in oak for 12 months, with the once firm tannins now integrated nicely with spicy wood and opening on the palate to reveal appealing wild red and black berries and cassis along with hints of minted chocolate. Generous and moderately long. Drink now. Score 89.

CHÂTEAU LA TONNELLE, CRU BOURGEOIS, HAUT-MÉDOC, 2005: Precisely what a cru bourgeois wine should be, a bit in the country style but with enough charm to carry it to a most pleasant level. Medium-bodied, with somewhat chunky tannins and spicy wood, opening in the glass to reveal wild berry and currant fruits, those supported nicely by hints of Oriental spices and baker's chocolate. Drink now–2011. Score 87.

CHÂTEAU LA TONNELLE, HAUT-MÉDOC, 2002: Dark garnet towards royal purple, medium- to full-bodied, with firm, mouth-coating tannins yielding slowly in the glass to reveal currant and wild berry fruits, those on a lightly spicy background. On the medium-long finish, hints of licorice. Drink now. Score 87.

CHÂTEAU LA TOUR SERAN, CRU BOURGEOIS, MÉDOC, 2005: Garnet towards royal purple, medium-bodied, with soft tannins and hints of spices and vanilla from the barriques in which it aged. On the nose and palate straightforward but appealing blackberry and black cherry fruits, those on a background of earthy minerals. Drink now–2012. Score 87.

CHÂTEAU LE CROCK, CRU BOURGEOIS, ST. ESTÈPHE, 2005: Dark garnet, full-bodied, with chewy tannins and notes of spicy and toasty oak. Opens to reveal fine blackcurrant, blackberry and chocolate notes and, on the moderately long finish, a hint of eucalyptus. Best kosher edition to date from this winery. Drink now–2014. Score 90.

CHÂTEAU LE CROCK, CRU BOURGEOIS, ST. ESTÈPHE, 2004: Full-bodied, garnet towards royal purple, with soft, gently mouth-coating tannins and opening to show forward blackberry, blueberry and licorice notes. Well balanced and long. Drink now–2013. Score 88.

CHÂTEAU LE CROCK, ST. ESTÈPHE, 2003: Dark garnet with purple and orange reflections, full-bodied, with still gripping tannins needing time to settle in. On the nose and palate blackberry, currant and black cherry fruits, those on a background of Oriental spices and olives. On the finish, hints of licorice and citrus peel. A blend of Cabernet Sauvignon, Merlot, Cabernet Franc and Petit Verdot (55%, 30%, 10% and 5% respectively). Drink now–2012. Score 89.

CHÂTEAU LE CROCK, ST. ESTÈPHE, 2002: As we have come to know, the signature of this Château, full-bodied, with firm tannins and generous spicy wood but those in good balance and opening in the glass to reveal currants, wild berries and hints of earthy-herbaceousness. Well crafted. Drink now–2011. Score 89.

CHÂTEAU LÉOVILLE POYFERRÉ, ST. JULIEN, 2005: Perhaps the

best kosher edition ever from Léoville Poyferré. A blend of 62% Cabernet Sauvignon, 28% Merlot, 8% Petit Verdot and 2% Cabernet Franc. Deep garnet towards royal purple in color, full-bodied, with gently caressing tannins and just the right hint of spicy and vanilla rich oak. On first attack, blackcurrants and blackberries, those followed by hints of blueberries and, on the long finish, notes of lightly minted chocolate. Approachable and enjoyable now but best from 2011. Score 92.

CHÂTEAU LÉOVILLE POYFERRÉ, ST. JULIEN, 2004: Full-bodied, with firm tannins starting to integrate with hints of spices and vanilla from the oak in which it aged. Opens to show traditional currant and blackberry fruits, those on a lightly spicy background. Best 2010–2014. Score 89.

CHÂTEAU LÉOVILLE POYFERRÉ, ST. JULIEN, 2003: Full-bodied, with good concentration and with its firm tannins starting to integrate and opening to reveal ripe currants, black cherries and purple plums, those on a background of toasty oak. Long and generous but needs time. Approachable and enjoyable now but best 2011–2015. Score 91.

CHÂTEAU LÉOVILLE POYFERRÉ, ST. JULIEN, 2001: Dark garnet, full-bodied, with softly caressing tannins and appealing spicy cedar overtones. On the nose and palate currant, wild berry and chocolate notes, all with a light overlay of cigar tobacco. Drink now–2015. Score 91.

CHÂTEAU LÉOVILLE POYFERRÉ, ST. JULIEN, 2000: Full-bodied and well balanced, with firm tannins and spicy wood integrating nicely now. On the nose and palate blackberries, currants, chocolate and *garrigue*, all leading to a generous and mouth-filling finish. Drink now–2015, perhaps longer. Score 92.

CHÂTEAU MALARTIC LAGRAVIÈRE, PESSAC-LÉOGNAN, 2004: Dark garnet, full-bodied, with silky tannins and a gentle hand with the oak. Fine balance and structure here as the wine reveals blackcurrant, blackberry and dark chocolate notes on first attack, those yielding comfortably to hints of cigar tobacco and freshly roasted herbs. Long and generous. Drink now–2015, perhaps longer. Score 90.

CHÂTEAU MALARTIC LAGRAVIÈRE, GRAND CRU CLASSÉ DE GRAVES, PESSAC-LÉOGNAN, 2003: Dark garnet towards royal purple, medium- to full-bodied, with soft tannins and notes of spicy oak. Opens in the glass to reveal blackberry, black cherry and tobacco notes and, on the long finish, Mediterranean herbs and a hint of red cherries. Drink now–2015. Score 89.

CHÂTEAU MALMAISON, BARONNE NADINE DE ROTHSCHILD, MOULIS, 2005: Deep, almost impenetrable garnet in color, full-bodied, with smooth tannins and opening in the glass to reveal currant, wild berry and citrus peel notes all leading to a long chocolate-rich finish. Best 2010–2020. Score 91.

CHÂTEAU MALMAISON, BARONNE NADINE DE ROTHSCHILD, MOULIS, 2003: Dark ruby towards garnet, full-bodied, with soft, mouth-coating tannins that are integrating nicely with spicy wood and, on the palate, black fruits, spices and, on the long finish, appealing hints of freshly turned earth. Drink now–2012. Score 89.

CHÂTEAU MALMAISON, BARONNE NADINE DE ROTHSCHILD, MOULIS, 2002: Garnet towards royal purple, medium-bodied, with near-sweet soft tannins integrated nicely. On the nose and palate ripe plums, berries and cassis, those with a light overlay of milk chocolate. Easy to drink. Drink now. Score 88.

CHÂTEAU MALMAISON, BARONNE NADINE DE ROTHSCHILD, MOULIS, 2001: Deep ruby red, medium- to full-bodied, with soft tannins and on the nose and palate wild berries, cassis and a hint of spices. A well-made wine but lacking depth or complexity. Drink now. Score 87.

CHÂTEAU MONTVIEL, POMEROL, 2004: A dark garnet, medium- to full-bodied red, with soft tannins integrated nicely. Neither complex nor long but with appealing plum, berry and tobacco aromas and flavors that make this a good quaffer. Drink now. Score 86.

CHÂTEAU PATRIS, FILIUS DE CHÂTEAU PATRIS, ST. EMILION, 2003: Dark ruby towards garnet, full-bodied, with somewhat chunky tannins that give the wine a country style, but given time this one promises to settle down nicely. On the nose and palate traditional currant, blackberry and blueberry fruits overlaid by spicy wood and appealing notes of asphalt and mint. Promises to be long and generous. Best now–2012. Score 90.

CHÂTEAU PATRIS, FILIUS DE CHÂTEAU PATRIS, ST. EMILION, 2000: Medium- to full-bodied, with soft tannins and a hint of spicy oak, those well integrated and showing generous blackberry and black cherry fruits. In the background, hints of white pepper and red licorice. Drink now–2012. Score 90.

CHÂTEAU PATRIS, ST. EMILION, 2000: Medium- to full-bodied, with soft tannins and a hint of spicy oak, those well integrated and showing generous blackberry and black cherry fruits. In the background, hints of white pepper and red licorice. Drink now–2012. Score 90.

CHÂTEAU PEYRAT-FOURTHON, HAUT-MÉDOC, 2003: Dark garnet, this traditional Bordeaux blend (55% Cabernet Sauvignon, 36% Merlot,

5% Cabernet Franc and 4% Petit Verdot) shows full-bodied, with soft, gently mouth-coating tannins and light hints of spicy wood highlighting blackcurrant and blackberry fruits, those complemented nicely by hints of bitter-sweet chocolate and tobacco. Long, round and generous. Drink now–2011, perhaps longer. Score 90.

CHÂTEAU PONTET-CANET, PAUILLAC, 2005: Whoever is "doing it" at Pontet-Canet is doing it very well indeed, and this kosher edition, although not quite the regular edition (which scores a generous 95 points) is just fine on its own. Dark, almost impenetrable garnet in color, full-bodied, with soft, gently mouth-coating tannins. On first attack currants and mint, those opening to reveal blackberry, licorice and mineral notes and, on the super-long finish, the tannins and fruits rising along with a generous note of espresso coffee. Approachable now, but best starting only in 2011 and then cellaring comfortably until 2025. Score 93.

CHÂTEAU PONTET-CANET, PAUILLAC, 2004: Medium- to full-bodied, showing traditional Cabernet Sauvignon blackberry and blackcurrant fruits, those complemented comfortably by hints of spices, minerals and licorice. Long and near-elegant. Best 2010–2015. Score 91.

CHÂTEAU PONTET-CANET, PAUILLAC, 2003: Deep ruby towards garnet, full-bodied, with soft tannins and notes of smoky wood that unfold to reveal generous red berry, red currant and licorice, those on a background of Oriental spices. Fruits and tannins rise comfortably on the long finish. Approachable and enjoyable now, but best 2010–2017. Score 90.

CHÂTEAU PONTET-CANET, PAUILLAC, 2002: Medium- to full-bodied, with soft tannins, generous wood and rich, ripe currant, blackberry and purple plums on a background of sweet cedar and minerals. Well balanced, round and mouth-filling. Drink now–2013. Score 91.

CHÂTEAU PONTET-CANET, PAUILLAC, 2001: Dark garnet in color, full-bodied, with soft tannins integrated nicely with light notes of spicy wood. On the nose and palate blackcurrants, blackberries and licorice. Shows fine balance and length. Drink now–2011. Score 89.

CHÂTEAU QUINAULT, ST. EMILION, 2005: The first kosher edition released from this Château, and certainly a winner. Dark, almost impenetrable ruby towards garnet in color, medium- to full-bodied, with gently mouth-coating tannins and a judicious hand with spicy oak. On first attack blackberries and cassis, those yielding to raspberries and black cherries, all on a background that hints of dark minted chocolate. Long and generous. Approachable and enjoyable now, but best 2011–2022. Score 93.

CHÂTEAU ROC DE BOISSAC, ST. EMILION, 2000: Dark garnet red, medium- to full-bodied, with firm tannins and generous wood tending to overpower the black fruits that are here. An appealing country-style wine. Drink now. Score 86.

CHÂTEAU ROLLAN DE BY, CRU BOURGEOIS, MÉDOC, 2003: Best ever from this winery, an often under-rated cru bourgeois producer and thus often a good buy. Garnet towards royal purple, medium- to full-bodied, with softly gripping tannins and gentle notes of spicy wood. On the nose and palate currant, berry and citrus peel notes and, on the long finish, the tannins rise with a hint of chocolate. Drink now–2012. Score 89.

CHÂTEAU ROLLAN DE BY, ROYALE RESERVE, MÉDOC, 2002: Far better this year than the regular (i.e., non-kosher) edition, an oak-aged blend of Merlot, Cabernet Sauvignon and Cabernet Franc (70%, 20% and 10% respectively). Medium- to full-bodied, with soft tannins nicely integrating and generous currant and blackberry aromas and flavors, those backed up by a generous hint of minerals and spices on the medium-long finish. Best now-2010. Score 87.

CHÂTEAU ROLLAN DE BY, MÉDOC, 2001: Medium-bodied, with chunky, country-style tannins, those integrating nicely with light toasty oak and generous berry, black cherry and plum fruits. Not complex but a fine match to food. Drink now. Score 87.

CHÂTEAU ROYAUMONT, LALANDE DE POMEROL, 2003: Dark ruby towards garnet, full-bodied, with chewy tannins and notes of spicy cedarwood. Opens in the glass to show a tempting array of red and black berries and cassis, on a background of earthy minerals and Mediterranean herbs. Drink now–2011. Score 89.

SARGET DE GRUAUD LAROSE, ST. JULIEN, 2000: This kosher edition of the second wine of Gruaud Larose is indeed a very good effort. Full-bodied, with once youthful and firm tannins now settling in nicely to show a tempting array of blackberries, purple plums and black cherries, those on a background of bitter-sweet chocolate. Notes of tobacco and vanilla rise on the long and generous finish. Drink now–2013. Score 91.

CHÂTEAU SMITH-HAUT-LAFITTE, BLANC, PESSAC-LÉOGNAN, 2004: Made entirely from Sauvignon Blanc grapes, this full-bodied wine shows appealing citrus and green apples along with generous hints of tropical fruits and spicy herbs. The only fault of the wine, its excess acidity, is also in an odd way a strength, as it gives the wine zip. That acidity does however rob the wine of its complexity. Drink now or in the next year or two. Score 87.

CHÂTEAU SMITH-HAUT-LAFITTE, PESSAC-LÉOGNAN, 2002: Medium- to full-bodied, with soft tannins and gentle toasty wood influences settling in nicely to reveal a complex array of blackberry, blackcurrant and cherry notes, those on a background of earthy-minerals and Oriental spices. An almost impenetrably dark royal purple in color and with a long and intense finish on which the tannins rise nicely. Drink now–2013. Score 90.

CHÂTEAU SMITH-HAUT-LAFITTE, PESSAC-LÉOGNAN, 2001: Full-bodied, with its once firm tannins now integrating nicely and showing generous blackberry, blueberry and cassis notes, those highlighted by notes of freshly turned earth and licorice. Drink now–2012. Score 90.

CHÂTEAU SMITH-HAUT-LAFITTE, PESSAC-LÉOGNAN, 2000: Medium-bodied with soft tannins integrating beautifully and a generous array of berry, currant and black cherry fruits backed up nicely by hints of bitter-sweet chocolate, espresso coffee and, on the long finish, a hint of cigar tobacco. One of the very best kosher releases of the vintage. Best 2006–2012, perhaps longer. Score 90.

CHÂTEAU TERTRE DAUGAY, ST. EMILION, 2000: Dark royal purple in color, full-bodied, with soft tannins and a gentle oak influence. Opens in the glass to reveal generous black and red berries and currants, those on a background of Oriental spices. Long and generous. Drink now–2014. Score 90.

CHÂTEAU TEYSSIER, ST. EMILION, 2002: Medium- to full-bodied, with still firm tannins opening to reveal blackcurrant and wild berry fruits, those on a background of lightly spicy wood. Drink now. Score 88.

CHÂTEAU TOUR SERAN, MÉDOC, 2000: Medium- to full-bodied, garnet towards royal purple in color, with soft, near-sweet tannins and hints of vanilla from the oak in which it aged. Opens to reveal straightforward but appealing plum, black cherry and raisined fruits on a light tarry background. Drink now. Score 87.

CHÂTEAU DE VALANDRAUD, ST. EMILION, 2005: Youthful dark royal purple in color, full-bodied, with soft tannins integrating nicely with notes of sweet cedarwood. On the nose and palate blackberry, currant and purple plums on a spicy background. Lingers long and generously on the palate. Drink now–2018. Score 90.

CHÂTEAU DE VALANDRAUD, ST. EMILION 2003: A lighter than usual Valandraud, but don't let that hold you back, for this medium- to full-bodied, softly tannic red shows appealing blackberry, blackcurrant and vanilla notes, those hinting of white pepper and Mediterranean herbs. On the generous finish, notes of black tea and licorice. Drink now–2012. Score 89.

CHÂTEAU DE VALANDRAUD, ST. EMILION, 2002: Garnet towards royal purple in color, medium-bodied, with once firm tannins now settling in comfortably to let the wine open to reveal plum, red currant and red berry fruits, those complemented by notes of exotic spices. Tannins rise together with a note of spicy wood on the generous finish. Drink now–2011. Score 89.

CHÂTEAU DE VALANDRAUD, ST. EMILION, 2001: Dark garnet towards royal purple, opens with firm tannins and super-generous smoky and spicy wood, but given time in the glass (or perhaps the decanter) opens to reveal that those tannins and wood are now integrating nicely, even softening on the palate, and revealing near-sweet plum, berry and cassis fruits along with hints of white chocolate. Long and generous. Drink now–2014. Score 92.

CHÂTEAU DE VALANDRAUD, VIRGINIE DE VALANDRAUD, ST. EMILION 2003: The second wine of Valandraud and a close match to the non-kosher release. Medium-bodied, with soft tannins and generous blackcurrant and blackberry fruits, those matched nicely by hints of sweet cedar and spring flowers. Drink now–2011. Score 88.

Chablis

PASCAL BOUCHARD, CHABLIS, 2006: Fresh, crisp and generous, with fine balancing acidity and flinty minerals highlighting apple, pear and citrus fruits. Drink now–2011. Score 88.

Rhone

DOMAINE ST. BENOIT, CHÂTEAUNEUF-DU-PAPE, LAURELINE, 2005: Garnet towards royal purple in color, medium- to full-bodied, with firm tannins only now starting to settle in. Opens slowly in the glass to reveal generous purple plum, blackcurrant and blackberry fruits, those supported by hints of spicy cedarwood and smoked meat. Drink now–2014. Score 88.

DOMAINE ST. BENOIT, CHÂTEAUNEUF-DU-PAPE, GRANDE GARDE, 2005: Garnet red, medium- to full-bodied, with firm tannins waiting to integrate with smoky wood, spices and earthiness. On the nose and palate floral notes and an array of red and black berries, black cherries and, on the moderately long finish, a hint of freshly tanned leather. Drink now–2012. Score 86.

Vin de Pays

HERZOG SELECTION, CABERNET SAUVIGNON, VIN DE PAYS D'OC, 2005: Ruby towards garnet in color, medium-bodied, a pleasant little country-style wine with generous berry, cherry and currant fruits. Drink now. Score 86.

HERZOG SELECTION, CABERNET SAUVIGNON, ORGANIC, VIN DE PAYS D'OC, 2004: Not fully organic but made from organically grown grapes. Medium- to full-bodied, with lightly gripping tannins and an appealing berry-cherry personality. Drink now. Score 86.

HERZOG SELECTION, MERLOT, VIN DE PAYS D'OC, 2005: Dark ruby towards garnet, medium-bodied, with soft tannins and generous herbal hints, opens to reveal black cherry, blackberry and light chocolate notes. Drink now. Score 86.

HERZOG SELECTION, SAUVIGNON BLANC, VIN DE PAYS D'OC, 2006: A pleasant little white wine, medium-bodied, straw colored, with lively acidity to set off pear, melon and citrus fruits, those supported by a note of freshly mowed grass. Drink now. Score 86.

CHÂTEAU MINISTRE, COTEAUX DU LANGUEDOC, 2004: Dark but not fully clear garnet in color, this blend of equal parts of Grenache and Syrah needs either decanting or about an hour to open in the glass before it begins to show its charms. Medium- to full-bodied, with firm, somewhat chunky tannins, but opening to reveal an appealing array of plums, cherries and spices, all finishing with generous hints of pepper and smoke. A most pleasant country-style wine. Drink now. Score 88.

ISRAEL

Alexander Winery ★★★★★

ALEXANDER THE GREAT, CABERNET SAUVIGNON, 2006: Dark garnet towards royal purple, full-bodied and with still firm tannins and reflecting its development in barriques for 15 months with generous spicy wood, those in fine balance and needing only time in the glass to integrate. On the nose and palate blackcurrant, blackberry and dark chocolate notes, all leading to a long mouth-filling finish. Drink now–2012. Score 89.

ALEXANDER, SYRAH, 2006: Deep garnet towards royal purple, medium- to full-bodied, with gently caressing tannins. On first attack hints of spices and peppery oak, those parting to reveal blackcurrant, wild berry and orange peel notes. Look as well for a hint of tar that rises nicely on the finish. Drink now–2011. Score 89.

Asif Winery ★★★★

ASIF, CABERNET SAUVIGNON-CABERNET FRANC-MERLOT, 2005: Garnet, full-bodied, with tannins integrating nicely with spicy wood. Oak-aged for 18 months, showing warm and round, with generous blackcurrant and blackberry fruits complemented nicely by notes of Oriental spices, black pepper and green olives. A blend of 85% Cabernet Sauvignon, 9% Cabernet Franc and 6% Merlot. Drink now, perhaps longer. Score 88.

Barkan Winery ✴✴✴

Superieur Series

CABERNET SAUVIGNON, SUPERIEUR, 2003:
Dark, almost impenetrable royal purple in color,
firm and concentrated, one of the best ever from
Barkan. Full-bodied, with gently mouth-coating
tannins and a judicious hand with spicy oak,
shows intense aromas and flavors of blackcurrants, blackberries and black cherries, those
complemented by hints of dates, sage and near-
sweet cedarwood. A long finish bursting with
minerals and black fruits. Drink now. Score 91.

MERLOT, SUPERIEUR, 2004: Medium- to full-
bodied, with soft tannins integrating nicely,
showing smoky blackberry, berry, black cherry
and cassis fruits, those on a light background of red peppers and vanilla,
all leading to a long, smooth, mouth-filling finish. Drink now. Score 89.

Reserve Series

MERLOT, RESERVE, 2006: Dark garnet, me-
dium- to full-bodied, with soft, near-sweet tannins and hints of spicy wood from the 14 months
it spent in new French barriques. Opens to show
blackberries and purple plums, those parting in
the glass to make way for red fruits, cassis and
notes of citrus peel. On the finish, hints of what
at one moment seem like mint, at the next of
licorice. Drink now–2011. Score 88.

SHIRAZ, RESERVE, 2006: Deep and youthful,
garnet towards royal purple in color, reflecting
its year in French and American barriques with
appealing spicy notes. Full-bodied, with gripping
tannins and a tempting note of bitter herbs that
runs through. Blended with 4% each of Cabernet
Sauvignon and Petit Verdot, opens to show appealing red berry and
cherry fruits, those complemented by hints of white pepper and licorice.
Drink now–2011. Score 88.

SAUVIGNON BLANC, RESERVE, 2006: With 20% of the wine aged
sur lie in new wood for three months and the remainder developed in

stainless steel, this light golden straw, medium-bodied white shows deeply aromatic with good balancing acidity. On the nose and palate tropical fruits, citrus peel and hints of Mediterranean herbs. Drink now. Score 88.

Altitude Series

CABERNET SAUVIGNON, ALTITUDE 624, 2005: Deep, almost impenetrable garnet in color, this medium- to full-bodied wine shows firm, drying tannins and spicy oak on first attack, those receding in the glass to add a near-sweetness to the black and red fruits, Oriental spices and hints of freshly picked mushrooms and green olives. Long and generous. Drink now. Score 90.

CABERNET SAUVIGNON, ALTITUDE 720, 2005: Opens with a smoky, spicy nose, and goes on to deliver appealing plum, blackberry and currant fruits, those overlaid with Oriental spices. Soft, caressing tannins and gentle wood add to the complexity of the wine. Look as well for a tantalizing hint of earthy bitterness that comes in on the long finish. Drink now–2013. Score 91.

Bashan Winery ✳✳✳

BASHAN, CABERNET SAUVIGNON, EITAN, 2005: Medium- to full-bodied, this organic wine shows good balance between sweet oak, generous yeasts and on the nose and palate appealing ripe and spicy black fruits. Drink now. Score 88.

Bazelet HaGolan Winery ✳✳✳

BAZELET HAGOLAN, CABERNET SAUVIGNON, RE-SERVE, 2005: Rich, ripe, smooth, generous and well balanced with currant, berry and plum flavors coming together with near-sweet tannins, and tempting smoky oak lingering nicely. Drink now–2012. Score 88.

BAZELET HAGOLAN, CABERNET SAUVIGNON, RESERVE, 2004: Dark garnet towards royal purple, full-bodied, with firm tannins in fine balance with acidity, spicy wood and fruits. On first attack, blackcurrants and black licorice, those followed by wild berries, earthy minerals and Mediterranean herbs. Long and generous. Drink now–2011. Score 90.

Benhaim Winery ✳✳✳

BENHAIM, CABERNET SAUVIGNON, RESERVE, 2006: Showing dark royal purple towards garnet, medium- to full-bodied, with generous soft tannins and abundant spicy and dusty oak. On the nose and palate blackcurrants, berries and plums, with light herbal and green olive overtones. Round and well balanced. Drink now–2011. Score 88.

Binyamina Winery ✳✳✳✳

Reserve Series

RESERVE, CABERNET SAUVIGNON, 2006: Dark garnet in color, deeply aromatic and showing full body and generous but comfortably yielding tannins, those in fine balance with fruits, wood and acidity. Reflecting oak-aging for 18 months with spicy overtones, and opening in the glass to reveal blackberry, currant and purple plum fruits, those supported nicely by hints of black pepper. Medium- towards full-bodied, mouth-filling and long. Drink now–2012. Score 90.

RESERVE, MERLOT, 2006: Full-bodied, reflecting its 14 months in oak with notes of vanilla and spices as well as a cigar-box note that runs through. On the nose and palate opens with strawberries and raspberries, those yielding comfortably to blackberries and currants, all with a generous peppery note that lingers nicely on the long finish. Give this one some time to develop in the bottle and it will show some licorice and smoked meat aromas and flavors as well. One of the best ever from Binyamina. Drink now–2013. Score 92.

RESERVE, SHIRAZ, 2006: Developed for 12 months in French and American oak, a full-bodied, dark garnet, aromatic Shiraz, blended, as seems to be the wont these days, with 2% of white Viognier grapes, this adding both liveliness and flavor. On the nose and palate light notes of smoky wood to match black and red berries, cherries and spices, the tannins coating the mouth gently and then lingering on the generously fruity finish. Drink now–2013. Score 91.

Avnei Hachosen Series

AVNEI HACHOSEN, CABERNET SAUVIGNON, TARSHISH, 2005: Dark garnet with purple and orange reflections, medium-bodied, aged in new French oak for 16 months. Opens with super-soft tannins, those firming as the wine develops in the glass, with appealing currant and red plums on the nose and palate, those backed up by a hint of sweet herbs on the moderately long finish. Drink now–2011. Score 89.

AVNEI HACHOSEN, SYRAH, ODEM, 2007: Full-bodied, soft, round and juicy, with a generous array of blueberries, blackberries, purple plums and a mélange of herbal and spicy notes that lead to a long finish. Drink now–2012. Score 89.

AVNEI HACHOSEN, SYRAH, ODEM, 2006: Dark, dense and concentrated, with fine balance and structure. Firm tannins now integrating nicely with spicy wood to show the black and red berries, cherries and licorice flavors that are here, lingering comfortably on a long fruity finish. Drink now–2013. Score 90.

AVNEI HACHOSEN, CABERNET SAUVIGNON-SHIRAZ-MERLOT, SAPIR, 2005: A blend of 40% Cabernet Sauvignon, 35% Shiraz and 25% Merlot. Oak-aged for 15 months, showing dark ruby towards garnet, opening with licorice and mint on the nose and palate, those going to bittersweet chocolate and Mediterranean herbs and then to red plums, cassis and spicy notes. Drink now. Score 89.

Yogev Series

BINYAMINA, CABERNET SAUVIGNON-PETIT
VERDOT, YOGEV, 2006: A medium-bodied,
softly tannic blend of 80% Cabernet Sauvignon
and 20% Petit Verdot, opening on the palate to
reveal gentle spicy wood and blackberry and
currant fruits, those complemented by a light
herbal note. Round and moderately long. Drink
now. Score 89.

Tiltan Series

יוגב

BINYAMINA, TILTAN, N.V.: A blend not of different grape varieties
but of Cabernet Sauvignon grapes from three different vintage years, in
this case, as noted on the front label, from 2004, 2005 and 2006. Developed in barriques for 18 months, showing generous but not offensive
sweet cedarwood and moderately gripping tannins that yield nicely
to show blackberry, blackcurrant and orange peel notes, all on a light
background of green olives and eucalyptus. Drink now–2011. Score 88.

BINYAMINA, TILTAN, N.V.: Made from Cabernet Sauvignon grapes
harvested in the 2003, 2004 and 2005 harvests, each developed in wood
for a different period of time. Full-bodied, with soft, caressing tannins
and a moderate hand with peppery wood, the wine opens on the palate
to reveal currants, black cherries and herbal aromas and flavors, all of
which are concentrated but not heavy. Finishes with generous tannins
and an appealing hint of sage. Drink now–2012. Score 90.

Bustan Winery ✶✶✶✶

BUSTAN, CABERNET SAUVIGNON, 2004:
Dark, almost impenetrable royal purple in
color, full-bodied and powerful, with soft,
mouth-coating tannins along with aromas
and flavors of blackcurrants, blackberries,
plums and spices, all with notes of chocolate, minerals and spicy cedarwood. Long
and generous. Drink now–2014. Score 91.

BUSTAN, CABERNET SAUVIGNON, 2003:
Dark ruby to garnet, medium-bodied, with
soft tannins integrating well and with

generous but not overwhelming spicy oak. Spicy currant and berry fruits along with chocolate and tobacco on the powerful but elegant finish. Drink now–2011. Score 90.

BUSTAN, SYRAH, 2005: Full-bodied, with super-soft tannins and opening with a burst of sweet and savory tannins, those parting in the glass to reveal layer after layer of blackberry, plum and citrus peel notes, complemented by notes of black tea, white pepper and, on the long finish, a hint of peppermint. Concentrated, intense, well focused, supple and harmonious, with a super-long finish. Drink now–2013. Score 92.

BUSTAN, SYRAH, 2004: Dark garnet, full-bodied, with firm tannins and gentle smoky wood influences. On the nose and palate black fruits, exotic spices and hints of saddle leather and earthy minerals. Long and generous. Drink now–2012. Score 90.

Carmel Winery★★★★

Limited Edition

LIMITED EDITION, 2007: Full bodied and concentrated but not at all bombastic, developed in Burgundy-sized barrels and showing fine balance and structure that bode well for the future. A blend of Cabernet Sauvignon, Petit Verdot, Merlot, Malbec and Cabernet Franc (57%, 31%, 5%, 5% and 2% respectively) showing a generous array of blackcurrant, blackberry and dark plum fruits, those supported by gentle notes of spicy oak and fresh acidity. Needs time for all of the elements to come together. Approachable now, but best 2011–2018. Score 93.

LIMITED EDITION, 2005: A Bordeaux blend of Cabernet Sauvignon, Petit Verdot, Merlot and Cabernet Franc (65%, 17%, 15% and 3% respectively). Dark ruby towards garnet, medium- to full-bodied, with generous soft tannins and reflecting its 15 months in barriques with light toasty and spicy oak. Blackberry and black cherry fruits on first attack, yielding to blackcurrants and appealing hints of lead pencil and vanilla and, on the moderately long finish, a near-sweet and elegant tobacco note. Drink now–2013. Score 92.

LIMITED EDITION, 2004: A blend of 65% Cabernet Sauvignon, 20% Petit Verdot and 15% Merlot, showing soft tannins and generous but gentle wood, those in fine balance with currant, blackberry and black cherry fruits, all melding together with light hints of pepper, anise and cigar box aromas and flavors. Round and caressing, elegant and long. Drink now–2013. Score 93.

Single Vineyard Series

SINGLE VINEYARD, CABERNET SAUVIGNON, KAYOUMI, UPPER GALILEE, 2007: Oak-aged for 15 months, a distinctive full-bodied Cabernet, showing cherry, raspberry and red currant fruits on a background of freshly turned earth and tobacco, all leading to a finish that goes on seemingly without end. Well focused and with excellent integration between fruits, tannins and wood. Drink now–2015. Score 93.

SINGLE VINEYARD, CABERNET SAUVIGNON, KAYOUMI, 2006: Super-dark garnet in color, with a traditional Cabernet nose, a long, round and concentrated wine, medium- to full-bodied with generous but gently mouth-coating tannins, opening to show currant, wild berry, chocolate and espresso coffee notes. Deep, round, nearly chewy and with a deep fruit finish. Drink now–2014. Score 91.

SINGLE VINEYARD, CABERNET SAUVIGNON, KAYOUMI, 2005: Dark garnet with green and orange reflections, full-bodied, open textured and generous, showing a spicy, peppery mouthful of blackberry, currant, coffee and black olive notes all leading to a long, round and mouth-filling finish. As this continues to develop, look for an appealing hint of smoked meat. Drink now–2013. Score 91.

SINGLE VINEYARD, CABERNET SAUVIGNON, KAYOUMI, 2004: Aged in oak for 15 months, the wine is dark, almost impenetrable purple in color. Firm tannins and smoky wood come together with currant, blackberry, plum and mineral aromas and flavors, those showing hints of Mediterranean herbs and light Oriental spices. Long and generous. Drink now–2012. Score 91.

SINGLE VINEYARD, CABERNET SAUVIGNON, KAYOUMI, 2003: Luscious and elegant, deep garnet, full-bodied and softly tannic. The nose and palate are still showing the blackcurrant, berry and spicy wood that were here but now these are complemented by hints of smoked meat, together with Oriental spices and tobacco. Long and complex. Drink now–2014. Score 92.

SINGLE VINEYARD, CABERNET SAU-VIGNON, ZARIT, 2004: Deep garnet towards royal purple, reflecting its 15 months in barriques with judicious oak integrating nicely with solid tannins. Opens with currants and dusty wood, moving on to spices and blackberries, and from first sip to last, hints of vanilla, freshly hung tobacco leaves and an intimation of mint. Long and generous. Drink now–2011. Score 91.

SINGLE VINEYARD, CABERNET SAUVIGNON, SCHECH, 2004: From a not-yet-well-known vineyard on the Golan Heights, this red lives up nicely to the stereotypes of what makes a wine "feminine." Soft, round and caressing, elegant without being intense, full-bodied without being muscular, with tempting aromas and flavors of black cherries, currants and anise. Drink now–2012. Score 90.

SINGLE VINEYARD, MERLOT, BEN ZIMRA, 2004: Dark towards inky garnet in color, full-bodied enough to be thought of as dense, with firm tannins integrating now to show fine structure and balance. Opens with a strong gamey aroma, but that fades quickly in the glass to reveal blackcurrants, purple plums and black olives, those highlighted by reined acidity and notes of tar and smoky oak. Long, with meaty flavors and fruits rising on the juicy finish. Drink now–2012. Score 91.

SINGLE VINEYARD, SHIRAZ, KAYOUMI, UPPER GALILEE, 2007: Almost impenetrably dark garnet in color, a big, bold and expressive wine, showing generous black cherry, red plum and raspberry fruits, those on a background of Oriental spices. Concentrated and mouth-filling, opening in layers on the palate and then lingering long and comfortably. Well crafted. Drink now–2015. Score 92.

SINGLE VINEYARD, SHIRAZ, KAYOUMI, 2005: Dark, almost impenetrable garnet, full-bodied, with silky tannins and showing fine balance and structure. Opens with a burst of dark plum and currant fruits, those yielding to notes of asphalt, bitter herbs and sweet-and-spicy cedarwood. Comes together as elegant, complex and long. Drink now–2012. Score 91.

SINGLE VINEYARD, SHIRAZ, KAYOUMI, 2004: Full-bodied, intense and concentrated, with soft tannins integrating nicely and showing layer after layer of spicy oak, smoked meat and tar, those highlighting red berries, black cherries and licorice. Drink now–2012. Score 91.

SINGLE VINEYARD, CHARDONNAY, KAYOUMI, 2006: With 75% developing in stainless steel and 25% in 300 liter Burgundy oak, this white is showing an aromatic Chablis-like personality, with minerals and light spices backing up hazelnuts, pears, figs and citrus. On the long finish a hint of toasted brioche. Drink now. Score 90.

SINGLE VINEYARD, JOHANNISBERG RIESLING, KAYOUMI, 2006: Bright and juicy, more off-dry than sweet, with tangy acidity highlighting green apple, grapefruit and mineral aromas and flavors. Good concentration in a medium-bodied wine that seems to float gently on the palate. Drink now. Score 89.

SINGLE VINEYARD, GEWURZTRAMINER, APPELLATION, UPPER GALILEE, 2008: An off-dry, unoaked white, made from grapes selected from the Kayoumi and Sha'al vineyards. Light gold with green tints, showing typical Gewurztraminer litchi and spicy notes, those matched nicely by notes of ripe peaches and apricots. Fine balancing acidity and a comfortably long finish. Drink now–2011, perhaps a bit longer. Score 90.

Appellation (Regional) Series

APPELLATION, CABERNET SAUVIGNON, UPPER GALILEE, 2007: Full-bodied, with silky tannins and generous but well-balanced spicy and vanilla-rich wood, those parting to reveal traditional blackcurrant and blackberry fruits, those complemented nicely by notes of grilled Mediterranean herbs. On the long finish generous fruits with a hint of near-sweet kirsch liqueur. Drink now–2012. Score 90.

APPELLATION, CABERNET SAUVIGNON, UPPER GALILEE, 2005: Blended with 7% Cabernet Franc, this firm, concentrated red shows bright, juicy currant and raspberry fruits, those with overlays of near-sweet cedarwood and sage and, on the long finish, a hint of licorice. Drink now. Score 89.

APPELLATION, MERLOT, UPPER GALILEE, 2006: Dark garnet towards royal purple, with soft tannins integrating nicely with spicy wood. Medium- to full-bodied, opens with a plum-rich nose, shifting on the palate to berry, black cherry and cassis fruits, all supported nicely by hints of white pepper and eucalyptus. Drink now–2011. Score 89.

CARMEL WINERY
—Since 1882—

APPELLATION

MERLOT
UPPER GALILEE

2006

APPELLATION, MERLOT, REGIONAL, UPPER GALILEE, 2005: Made from old vine Merlot blended with 7–10% of Cabernet Franc, this medium- to full-bodied wine shows soft, near-sweet tannins integrating nicely, and tempting aromas and flavors of ripe berries, plums, chocolate and licorice. Rich, round and delicious. Drink now. Score 89.

APPELLATION, CARIGNAN, OLD VINES, ZICHRON YA'AKOV, 2007: Made from thirty-year-old vines, blended with 10% Petit Verdot, oak-aged in minimal new oak for 14 months. Dark garnet, a fruit-forward blend showing blackcurrant, vanilla and violet notes on a background of fine tannins. Full-bodied, with abundant fruits and fine balance, needs a bit of time for the elements to come together. Best starting in 2011. Score 91.

APPELLATION, CARIGNAN, OLD VINES, ZICHRON YA'AKOV, 2006: A super-dark garnet blend of 85% Carignan and 15% Petit Verdot, the Carignan from 35–40-year-old, very low-yield, non-irrigated vines. A blockbuster on first attack, with the firm tannins and generous wood settling down to reveal a rich array of plum, red cherry, raspberry and currant fruits supported by hints of cocoa and spices and leading to a generous mocha-rich finish. Drink now–2011. Score 90.

APPELLATION, CARIGNAN, OLD VINES, ZICHRON YA'AKOV, 2005: Blended with 10% Petit Verdot and oak-aged for 12 months. Medium- to full-bodied, with soft, caressing tannins and spicy wood in fine balance with blackberry, cherry and peppery chocolate aromas and flavors, those leading to a medium-long espresso-rich finish. Drink now–2011. Score 91.

APPELLATION, CABERNET FRANC, UPPER GALILEE, 2007: From the Netua and Alma vineyards in the Upper Galilee, was developed for ten months in oak, some new and some used. Blended with 8% of Petit Verdot and 7% of Malbec, a medium- to full-bodied, deep garnet wine, showing soft tannins and gentle spicy oak influences integrating nicely, and opening to show red fruits and vanilla as well as a clear cigar box note. Drink now–2012. Score 90.

APPELLATION, PETITE SIRAH, OLD VINES, JUDEAN HILLS, 2007: Aged for 14 months in oak, partly new, partly used, made from 35-year-old vines, a concentrated and full-bodied red, showing royal purple in color and with generous tannins in fine balance with spicy and vanilla-rich wood. On the nose and palate a fine array of red and black fruits, those complemented by notes of black pepper, olives and Mediterranean herbs. Drink now–2013. Score 90.

APPELLATION, PETITE SIRAH, OLD VINES, JUDEAN HILLS, 2006: A big wine, full-bodied, deep garnet towards royal purple, oak-aged for 12 months, with gripping tannins just starting to settle down but showing fine balance between the tannins, wood and fruits. Ripe plum, blackberry and boysenberry notes on a background of minerals, minted chocolate and spicy cedarwood. Drink now–2012. Score 90.

APPELLATION, PETITE SIRAH, REGIONAL, JUDEAN HILLS, 2005: Developed in French oak for 12 months, made from grapes from 35-year-old vines, this almost impenetrably dark purple, still firmly tannic wine opens in the glass to reveal a rich array of dark plum, blueberry, peppery, herbal and spicy cedar notes. Dense enough to be thought of as chewable but opens to show harmony and grace. Drink now–2012. Score 91.

APPELLATION, CABERNET SAUVIGNON-SHIRAZ, UPPER GALILEE, 2007: A blend of equal parts of Cabernet Sauvignon and Shiraz, those developed for 12 months in 30% new barriques, showing gentle sweet and spicy oak. With the Shiraz clearly dominant, showing full-bodied with soft tannins, and opening to reveal red and black berries, plums and a hint of saddle leather. Finishes long and spicy. Drink now–2012. Score 90.

APPELLATION, SAUVIGNON BLANC, UPPER GALILEE, 2007: With only 7% of the wine aged in new 300 liter French barrels and the rest cold fermented and developed in stainless steel, the wine guards the varietal nature of the grape. Bright and lively, with passion fruit, pink grapefruit, green apple and just-tart-enough citrus fruits. Drink now. Score 89.

APPELLATION, VIOGNIER, UPPER GALILEE, 2008: With 25% of the wine developed in oak, the rest in stainless steel, some of the grapes early harvested and others late harvested, this is a ripe, creamy, near full-bodied white, showing concentrated citrus, pear and green apple notes, those on a background of dried apricots and, even though crisply dry, a tantalizing honeyed note. Drink now–2012. Score 90.

APPELLATION, JOHANNISBERG RIESLING, APPELLATION, UPPER GALILEE, 2008: Unoaked, medium-bodied, with fine aromatics. Categorized as off-dry but with a hint of sweetness so gentle that in Germany the wine would be labeled as *trocken* (i.e., dry). On the palate generous green apple, grapefruit, lemon curd, minerals and a nice hint of white pepper to add to its charm. Drink now–2012. Score 91.

APPELLATION, JOHANNISBERG RIESLING, REGIONAL, UPPER GALILEE, 2007: Late harvested, having undergone cold fermentation and developed entirely in stainless steel. Opens with a petrol-rich nose, that going on to reveal green apple, lemon custard and mineral flavors and aromas, all leading to a rich pink-grapefruit finish. Off-dry but with good balancing acidity. Drink now. Score 89.

Domaine du Castel *****

Grand Vin Castel

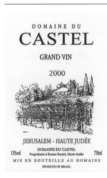

GRAND VIN CASTEL, 2007: Full-bodied, with gently caressing tannins and notes of spicy oak that part to make way for blackcurrant, blackberry and blueberry fruits, those supported by notes of mocha, orange peel and a delicate note of black olives that comes in on the long finish. Long, generous and coherent. Drink now–2016. Score 92.

GRAND VIN CASTEL, 2006: Cabernet Sauvignon and Merlot, those flushed out with Petit Verdot and Malbec. Firm, solid and intense, dark garnet in color, full-bodied, and opening to show a generous array of blackberries, black cherries, currants and dark chocolate. Dense, rich and complex, with hints of near-sweetness that play comfortably on the palate, with gently gripping tannins and in fine balance with wood and fruits. Long and generous, destined to be muscular and intense but with a distinct note of elegance. Drink now–2015. Score 93.

GRAND VIN CASTEL, 2005: Dark towards inky garnet with firm tannins now integrating nicely with spicy and smoky oak. Opens slowly in the glass to show a nose and palate of blackcurrant, blackberry and purple plum fruits on a background of generous Mediterranean herbs and near-sweet tobacco. On the long finish, hints of citrus peel, anise and dark chocolate. Drink now–2013. Score 92.

Petit Castel

PETIT CASTEL, 2006: A blend of Merlot, Petit Verdot and Cabernet Sauvignon. On first attack green and herbal notes, with cedary oak and tobacco flavors dominating, but then opening in the glass to show currants, purple plum and sage notes, the tannins rising on the finish. Drink now–2013. Score 89.

PETIT CASTEL, 2005: A blend primarily of Merlot, supplemented by Cabernet Sauvignon. Aged in oak for 16 months, this appealing dark red-ruby aromatic wine opens with red berries and spices, going on to black cherries, licorice and chocolate. Generous and with a tantalizing hint of sweetness on the long finish. Drink now–2011. Score 91.

PETIT CASTEL, 2004: Medium- to full-bodied and with soft tannins, this caressing red opens with a chocolate and berry-rich nose, joined by cassis, black cherries, dark plums, bittersweet chocolate and pepper, all lingering on a long, polished and round finish. Elegant and supple. Drink now. Score 92.

"C" Chardonnay

"C", CHARDONNAY, BLANC DU CASTEL, 2007: Gold, with green and orange tints, deeply floral, full-bodied and with generous but not overpowering oak that parts comfortably to reveal a complex array of citrus peel, summer fruits, hazelnuts, vanilla and crisp minerals. Lively and complex, opening nicely at this stage and showing a near creamy personality, that with a most welcome note of bitterness to enchant. Drink now–2011. Score 90.

"C", CHARDONNAY, BLANC DU CASTEL, 2005: Bright gold, full-bodied and concentrated, with light but not imposing buttery and spicy sensations. Rich, complex and opulent, with layers of citrus, figs, pears, summer fruits and toasty oak. Shows finesse and elegance. Drink now. Score 92.

The Cave ★★★★

THE CAVE, CABERNET SAUVIGNON-MERLOT, 2005: Full-bodied, with soft tannins integrating nicely and showing a moderate dose of spicy cedarwood, all in fine balance with fruits and acidity. A blend of 65% Cabernet Sauvignon and 35% Merlot, those vinified separately before the final blend was made near bottling time. Dark garnet towards royal purple in color, with currant, blackberry, spices and hints of bitter orange peel all coming together as a long and coherent whole. Drink now–2011. Score 90.

Dalton Winery ★★★★

Single Vineyard Series

SINGLE VINEYARD, CABERNET SAUVIGNON, MERON, 2004: Deep youthful cherry towards garnet, medium- to full-bodied, this well-balanced wine was aged in French oak for eight months and then bottled without filtration. Generous soft

tannins and ample wood, those already integrating nicely to reveal a very appealing array of red currant, raspberry and citrus peel on a peppery, lightly herbal, minty background. Round, long and mouth-filling. Drink now. Score 92.

SINGLE VINEYARD, MERLOT, MERON, 2005: Supple, rich and generous. Aged in oak for 16 months, with soft, near-sweet, mouth-coating tannins and fine balancing acidity to add liveliness to the blueberry and currant fruits. Hints of spices and mint run through to the long finish. Ripe, round and polished. Drink now–2011. Score 91.

Reserve Series

RESERVE, CABERNET SAUVIGNON, 2006: Super-dark garnet in color, firmly tannic but with fine balance and structure. A full-bodied, rich and concentrated wine, with dense fruit, coffee hints on the oak, and layers of currants, spices, green olives and cedarwood. Drink now–2014. Score 92.

RESERVE, CABERNET SAUVIGNON, 2005: Dark garnet with orange and green reflections, medium- to full-bodied, with still firm tannins integrating nicely and showing light spicy oak. Opens with currants and plums, goes on to wild berries and hints of black licorice and chocolate. Long, round and generous. Drink now. Score 91.

RESERVE, MERLOT, 2006: Dark, youthful royal purple in color, full-bodied, with soft, gently mouth-coating tannins integrating nicely with light spices and vanilla from the oak in which it is aging. Opens to reveal ripe and generous red plum, raspberry and coffee aromas and flavors, those supported nicely by a tantalizing hint of cigar tobacco. Long, ripe and generous. Drink now–2013. Score 90.

RESERVE, MERLOT, 2004: Medium- to full-bodied, with tannins that have firmed up somewhat but still remain in fine balance with wood, acidity and fruits. On the nose and palate, generous red and black berries and ripe red plums on a light tobacco and herbal background. Look as well for an appealing hint of vanilla that creeps in on the finish. Drink now–2011. Score 90.

RESERVE, SYRAH, 2005: Blended with 10% of Viognier, nearly black in color, but a wine of remarkable elegance. Aromatic, with spicy and floral scents on first attack, those yielding to aromas and flavors of berries and plums, all backed up by hints of white pepper, and, on the long finish, surprising notes of peaches and apricots. Drink now. Score 91.

RESERVE, SHIRAZ, 2004: Full-bodied and concentrated, with soft tannins and generous but not overpowering sweet cedar and spices from the barriques in which it aged. Aromas and flavors open with raspberries and go on to cherries, berries, red plums, pepper and an attractive earthiness. Generous and long. Drink now. Score 90.

RESERVE, SAUVIGNON BLANC, 2007: Unoaked, developed on its lees in stainless steel tanks, a crisp, lively and just-complex-enough wine. Lovely fruit here, with grapefruit running through but also showing citrus peel and a hint of grassiness on a light mineral background. Drink now. Score 89.

RESERVE, VIOGNIER, 2007: Perhaps the Israeli Viognier most loyal to the grape to date. Fermented partly with wild yeasts, developing in barriques on its lees, showing intense, vibrant and complex with spice, floral, fig and melon aromas and flavors. Deep and rich with a long, broad finish. Drink now–2011. Score 91.

Dalton Estate Series

ESTATE, CABERNET SAUVIGNON, 2007: Not a complex wine but very nice indeed, showing ripe and distinctive for cherry, blackberry, plum and herbal aromas and flavors framed by notes of sweet-and-spicy oak. Medium-bodied, with soft tannins, and lingering nicely on the palate. Drink now. Score 90.

ESTATE, MERLOT, 2007: Garnet towards royal purple, medium-bodied and generously aromatic, showing soft, well-integrated tannins and lightly spicy oak. On the nose and palate wild berries, currants and a hint of white chocolate on the long, round finish. Drink now. Score 88.

ESTATE, SHIRAZ, 2007: A distinctly New World wine, fruit-forward, medium- to full-bodied, with generous but not-at-all overpowering oak and soft tannins in fine balance. At first sip a virtual attack of berry and plum fruits, those yielding on the palate to blackberries and peaches along with an array of spices. Long and generous. Drink now–2012. Score 90.

ESTATE, FUMÉ BLANC, 2007: With a light note of oak, refreshing acidity and an appealing floral note on both nose and palate. On first attack grapefruit, peach and nectarine fruits, those turning towards papaya and mango. Crisp and refreshing, with a rich, smooth texture. Drink now. Score 89.

Alma Series

ALMA, 2005: Garnet towards purple, medium- to full-bodied, this blend of 65% Cabernet Sauvignon and 35% Merlot spent 16 months in French oak. Firm tannins integrating nicely with spicy oak. On the nose and palate blackberries, purple plums and a teasing hint of bitter oranges, the fruits backed up nicely by Oriental spices. Still firm tannins, spicy oak and acidity in fine balance. Drink now. Score 89.

ALMA, ZINFANDEL, 2006: Faithful to the variety, with full-body, wild berries, plums, vanilla and notes of white chocolate and cinnamon, all with a bare and tantalizing hint of sweetness. Aged in new American barriques for twelve months, showing fine balance between sweet and spicy oak, notes of black pepper, soft tannins and fruits. Drink now–2011. Score 90.

Ella Valley Vineyards ★★★★

Vineyards Choice Series

VINEYARDS CHOICE, CABERNET SAUVIGNON, 2007: Rich and ripe, full-bodied with near-sweet tannins and a judicious hand with spicy oak. Blended with 10% Merlot and 5% Petite Sirah, opens with a nose of freshly turned damp earth and plums, those yielding in the glass to aromas and flavors of ripe currants, blueberries, dark cherries and roasted Mediterranean herbs. Long and generous. Drink now–2015. Score 91.

VINEYARDS CHOICE, CABERNET SAUVIGNON, 2005: Full-bodied, with moderately firm tannins, a gentle wood influence, and fine balance. Blended with 10% of Merlot, this soft, round wine opens with near-sweet berries and spices, those yielding to reveal lush currant and blackberry aromas and flavors. Drink now–2013. Score 91.

VINEYARDS CHOICE, CABERNET SAUVIGNON, RR, 2004: Deep garnet towards royal purple in color, aged in French oak for 17 months, showing fine balance between spicy wood, soft tannins that are integrating nicely and fruits. On the nose and palate blackcurrants, purple plums and blackberries, those supported by gentle notes of white pepper and Mediterranean herbs. An elegant wine. Drink now–2014. Score 91.

VINEYARDS CHOICE, MERLOT, 2005: Deep and dark, with blockbuster tannins that promise to soften with time to show the wine's complexity and balance. A tempting array of black cherry, blackberry and currant flavors all coming together in a long finish. Drink now–2012. Score 91.

VINEYARDS CHOICE, SYRAH, 2007: Notably dark garnet in color, full-bodied, with fine balance between still gripping tannins and wood, and just waiting patiently for all of its elements to come together. On first attack currants, wild berries and an appealing loamy note, those opening to reveal hints of bay leaves, juniper berries and mint, all leading to a long and intense finish. Best 2010–2016. Score 92.

VINEYARDS CHOICE, CABERNET SAUVIGNON-MERLOT, 2005: Dark garnet towards purple, deeply aromatic, a full-bodied blend of 60% Cabernet Sauvignon and 40% Merlot. Muscular and tannic at this time but with fine balance and structure. Currant, cherry and berry fruits with generous hints of toasty oak on an appealing base of exotic spices. Overtones of cedar come in on the long finish. Drink now–2012. Score 90.

VINEYARDS CHOICE, MERLOT-CABERNET FRANC, 2006: A full-bodied blend of 80% Merlot and 20% Cabernet Franc, dark ruby towards garnet in color, and reflecting its time in oak with Oriental spices and firm tannins. Opens nicely in the glass to reveal blackberry, raspberry and dried currant fruits. Generously spicy, with a tantalizing hint of red chili rising on the super-long finish. Drink now–2013. Score 92.

Ella Valley Vineyards Series

ELLA VALLEY VINEYARDS, CABERNET SAUVIGNON, 2006: Medium- to full-bodied, with soft, gently mouth-coating tannins and gently spicy wood reflecting its 14 months in oak. A blend of 86% Cabernet Sauvignon and 14% Merlot showing currants, berries and hints of pepper, all leading to an aromatic and fruity finish. Drink now–2012. Score 90.

ELLA VALLEY VINEYARDS, MERLOT, 2007: Blended with 15% Cabernet Sauvignon, opens with a hint of dusty wood and near-sweet tannins. A full-bodied and firm Merlot showing round and well balanced, the tannins complemented nicely by light spicy oak. On the nose and palate generous blackberry, currant, wild berry and exotic spices, along with notes of minerals. Drink now–2013. Score 90.

ELLA VALLEY VINEYARDS, MERLOT, 2006: Full-bodied, a solid, almost muscular wine, but with gently gripping tannins in fine balance with spicy wood. Dark ruby towards garnet, showing a tempting array of raspberries, cherries and spices on a tempting earthy-mineral overlay. Long and generous. Drink now–2011. Score 90.

ELLA VALLEY VINEYARDS, SYRAH, 2007: Dark royal purple, full-bodied, with soft, gently gripping tannins and a generous mouthful of red plum, wild berry and boysenberry fruits, those complemented nicely by hints of peppery, spicy notes. Savory, intense and concentrated, but harmonious and elegant with a long spicy finish. Drink now–2012. Score 90.

ELLA VALLEY VINEYARDS, SYRAH, 2006: Blended with 3% each of Merlot and Cabernet Sauvignon, dark, almost inky-garnet in color, medium- to full-bodied, deeply aromatic and showing a generous array of blackberry, black cherry and currant notes. Long and mouth-filling. Drink now–2012. Score 92.

ELLA VALLEY VINEYARDS, PINOT NOIR, 2006: Dark cherry red, medium-bodied, with soft, well-integrating tannins and appealing raspberry, red plum and cherry flavors supported by sweet spices. Gains intensity in the glass and ends with a long finish. Drink now–2011. Score 90.

ELLA VALLEY VINEYARDS, PINOT NOIR, 2005: Ruby towards garnet in color, medium-bodied, with soft, caressing tannins and generous cherry, cassis, strawberry and cranberry aromas and flavors, those backed up nicely by minerals, hints of white pepper and vibrant acidity. Drink now–2012. Score 92.

ELLA VALLEY VINEYARDS, CABERNET FRANC, 2007: Dark, youthful royal purple in color at this stage, medium- to full-bodied, with soft, gently mouth-coating tannins. Rich and distinctive with light peppery and licorice hints running through the cherry and blackberry fruits. Look for hints of smoky oak on the long finish. Drink now–2012. Score 89.

ELLA VALLEY VINEYARDS, CABERNET FRANC, 2006: Developed in one- and two-year-old barrels and blended with 5% Merlot. Medium- to full-bodied, garnet towards royal purple with green and orange reflections, with blackberry and black cherry fruits overlaid with notes of rose petals. Opens slowly to reveal light tobacco and leathery notes, those on a background of crisp minerals. Tannins rise on the long finish to give grip to this elegant wine. Drink now–2013. Score 92.

ELLA VALLEY VINEYARDS, PETITE SIRAH, 2007: The winery's first release of a Petite Sirah varietal wine and quite a success. Made from grapes from ten-year-old vines, intensely dark royal purple in color, showing generous tannins and fine fruit concentration. On the nose and palate blackberries, raspberries and loganberry fruits, those matched nicely with notes of mint and tobacco. Firm and chewy with a long, near muscular finish. Drink now–2012. Score 90.

ELLA VALLEY VINEYARDS, CHARDONNAY, 2007: Developed partly in barriques, partly in stainless steel, promising to be a medium-bodied, crisply fresh and aromatic wine. Golden straw in color, showing a gentle hand with the wood, with the nose and palate opening with hints of honey, flaky pastry and minerals, and going on to show yellow plum and citrus blossoms. Well structured, long and elegant. As the wine develops in bottles look for a gentle honeyed hint that will creep in. Drink now–2011. Score 90.

ELLA VALLEY VINEYARDS, SAUVIGNON BLANC, 2007: Light straw in color, a bright and lively wine with pear, passion fruit and grapefruit showing nicely on the nose and palate and with a modicum of floral, anise and sage notes in the background. Fresh and appealing. Drink now. Score 89.

Galil Mountain Winery ✵✵✵✵

Yiron Series

GALIL MOUNTAIN, YIRON, 2005: A Bordeaux-plus wine—that is to say, 50% Cabernet Sauvignon, 44% Merlot and 2% Petit Verdot, plus 4% Syrah. Full-bodied and concentrated but simultaneously soft and elegant, with generous cassis and black fruits, velvety tannins and reflecting its 16 months in French oak with gently spicy and dusty wood, all of which lead to a super-long finish. Perhaps the best to date from the winery. Drink now–2015. Score 93.

GALIL MOUNTAIN, YIRON, 2004: A blend of 72% Cabernet Sauvignon, 25% Merlot and 3% Syrah. Intense garnet towards royal purple, full-bodied, with firm, near-sweet tannins integrating nicely with smoky and vanilla-tinged wood. Opens with wild berries on the nose and palate, those yielding to black cherry, cassis and spices, and finally on the long finish a tantalizing hint of bitterness. Drink now–2013. Score 91.

GALIL MOUNTAIN, SYRAH, YIRON, 2005: Dark, almost inky-garnet in color, medium- to full-bodied, with fine balance between soft tannins, spicy wood and fruits. On first attack raspberries and chocolate, those yielding to blackberries, currants and a rich floral note. On the long finish the tannins rise along with fruits and an appealing hint of red licorice. Drink now–2013. Score 91.

GALIL MOUNTAIN, SYRAH, YIRON, 2004: Dark royal purple with orange and green reflections, opening with a rich fruity and floral nose. Full-bodied, with bold but soft tannins integrating nicely with spicy wood and showing black fruits, dusty wood and light meaty and earthy overlays. Long and deep. Drink now–2012. Score 91.

Galil Mountain

GALIL MOUNTAIN, CABERNET SAUVIGNON, 2006: Super-dark garnet, showing moderate spicy and vanilla notes and soft, near-sweet tannins. On the nose and palate blackberries and blueberries, currants and, coming in from mid-palate, hints of earthiness and freshly turned mushrooms. Drink now. Score 90.

GALIL MOUNTAIN, CABERNET SAUVIGNON, 2005: Deep garnet with orange reflections, medium- to full-bodied, with appealing near-sweet tannins integrating nicely to reveal aromas and flavors of blackcurrants, wild berries and minerals all lingering nicely on the palate. Drink now. Score 89.

GALIL MOUNTAIN, MERLOT, 2006: Dark ruby towards garnet, medium- to full-bodied, with firm tannins settling in nicely now. On the nose and palate an array of red and black berry, purple plum and orange peel notes, those on a light background of Mediterranean herbs. Drink now. Score 90.

GALIL MOUNTAIN, SHIRAZ, 2007: Medium- to full-bodied, oak aged for 13 months, with gently mouth-coating tannins and showing an appealing array of cherry, wild berry and peppery notes, with a hint of bitter almonds on the long finish. Drink now–2011. Score 89.

GALIL MOUNTAIN, PINOT NOIR, 2007: Developed in one- to three-year-old French barrels, those imparting gentle spicy and vanilla notes.

Dark cherry red, medium-bodied, with soft tannins integrating nicely and opening to reveal red and black berries, cherries and earthy minerals. Soft and round, with just enough complexity to keep our attention. Score 88.

GALIL MOUNTAIN, PINOT NOIR, 2006: Dark cherry red towards garnet, medium-bodied, with its once firm tannins now settling in nicely. Opens to show a complex array of red berries, cherries, blueberries and spices, those supported nicely by light toasty vanilla and, on the finish, a hint of minerality. Drink now. Score 89.

GALIL MOUNTAIN, BARBERA, 2007: Reflecting its nine months in French oak with notes of smoky oak, medium-dark garnet in color, opening with a quiet nose but going on to reveal a generous array of berries, black cherries, purple plums and spring flowers. Tannins and oak rise along with a hint of bitter almonds on the finish, so give this one a bit of time in the glass for its elements to come together. Drink now–2013. Score 89.

GALIL MOUNTAIN, BARBERA, 2006: Developed for nine months in French oak, dark, almost inky ruby towards garnet in color, with its impressive 15% alcohol content in fine balance with wood, tannins and fruit. On the nose and palate blackberries, blueberries, plums and violets supported nicely by notes of vanilla, milk chocolate and, rising on the long finish, notes of black pepper. Gently mouth-coating tannins and fine concentration. Drink now–2011. Score 91.

GALIL MOUNTAIN, SHIRAZ-CABERNET SAUVIGNON, 2007: A blend of 51% Shiraz and 49% Cabernet Sauvignon, aged in American oak for ten months. Deep garnet towards royal purple, with generous but soft and gently mouth-coating tannins and fine concentration. Opens to reveal a medium- to full-bodied wine with plum, berry and cassis notes on a lightly spicy smoked-meat background. Drink now–2012. Score 88.

GALIL MOUNTAIN, CHARDONNAY, 2008: Lightly oaked, with a lively golden color, opens with a distinct peachy nose and goes on to show appealing citrus, apple and white peach fruits, all with a fine overlay of minerality. Look as well for a note of peach and cherry pits that comes in on the finish. Drink now–2010. Score 89.

GALIL MOUNTAIN, CHARDONNAY, 2007: Developed partly in oak, partly in stainless steel vats. Golden straw in color, medium-bodied, with a gentle hint of spicy oak and showing citrus, apple and pear fruits, those with a tempting hint of bitterness that creeps in on the finish. Drink now. Score 88.

GALIL MOUNTAIN, SAUVIGNON BLANC, 2008: An unoaked white, light straw in color, with a generously aromatic nose and crisply refreshing acidity, showing a tempting array of melon, citrus and kiwi fruits, those on a background that hints nicely of freshly mown grass. Drink now. Score 88.

GALIL MOUNTAIN, VIOGNIER, 2008: Developed in new French oak barrels, with a light, toasted white bread overlay. Light golden straw in color, with fine balancing acidity to highlight citrus and summer fruits, those hinting of a buttery overlay and peach pits. Medium-bodied but seems to float comfortably on the palate and finishing generous and long. Drink now–2011. Score 90.

GALIL MOUNTAIN, AVIVIM, 2007: Medium-bodied, light golden straw in color, a blend of 69% Viognier and 31% Chardonnay, those aged on their lees in new French oak barriques for nine months. Youthful and zesty, with lightly spicy cedarwood notes highlighting an array of tropical fruits, pears and honeydew melon. Lurking comfortably in the background a hint of red grapefruit. Drink now. Score 90.

Golan Heights Winery ✶✶✶✶✶

Katzrin

KATZRIN, 2004: Dark garnet towards royal purple, with orange and violet reflections. Shows generous oak and still firm tannins, those in fine proportion and well balanced by blackberry, blackcurrant and cherry fruits, on a background of white pepper, Mediterranean herbs and, on the long and generous finish, hints of vanilla and peppermint. Drink now–2016. Score 92.

KATZRIN, 2003: Dark garnet, a full-bodied blend of 83% Cabernet Sauvignon, 14% Merlot and 3% Cabernet Franc, with gently mouth-coating tannins and smoky oak integrating nicely. Shows layers of blackcurrant, black cherry and berry fruits, those yielding and coming together with peppery and herbal aromas and flavors culminating in a long blueberry and white chocolate finish. Best 2011–2018. Score 93.

KATZRIN, 2000: A blend of 89% Cabernet Sauvignon, 9% Merlot and 2% Cabernet Franc. Showing beautifully now, its blackberry, cherry and currant fruits supported by spicy oak, notes of cigar tobacco and hints of freshly turned earth. Dense, deep and intense, with finely tuned balance and structure, a simultaneously bold and elegant wine. Drink now–2015. Score 92.

KATZRIN, CHARDONNAY, 2004: Dark golden-yellow, full-bodied and concentrated. Developed in new oak for ten months, notably yeasty on first attack but that yielding beautifully to a buttery, oak-rich texture and opening to reveal nuts, fig, pear, tropical fruits and butterscotch, all on a spicy background. Rich, long and complex. Drink now–2012. Score 92.

KATZRIN, CHARDONNAY, 2003: Rich, ripe, concentrated and complex with generous layers of figs, tangerines, summer fruits and hazelnuts. Generous but not imposing oak on the finish makes it especially elegant, as does a hint of butterscotch that comes in on the long finish. Drink now. Score 92.

Yarden Series

YARDEN, CABERNET SAUVIGNON, ELROM VINEYARD, 2006: Full-bodied, with firm, near-sweet tannins and spicy oak integrating nicely. On the nose and palate currants, berries and spices, those opening to light earthy-herbal aromas and flavors. Tannins and fruits rise on the finish. Best from 2011–2016. Score 92.

YARDEN, CABERNET SAUVIGNON, 2006: Full-bodied, with soft tannins and spicy oak integrating nicely. On the nose and palate ripe black and red berries and currants on a background of spicy oak, all touched with hints of spices, vanilla and light mineral-earthy overtones. Drink now–2015. Score 91.

YARDEN, CABERNET SAUVIGNON, 2005: Brooding dark ruby-red, full-bodied, with near-sweet tannins and spicy oak wrapped around blackcurrants, berries, spices and a hint of dark chocolate. Look as well for enchanting hints of citrus peel and vanilla on the long finish. Fine balance and structure bode well for the future. Drink now–2018. Score 92.

YARDEN, CABERNET SAUVIGNON, ELROM VINEYARD, 2004: Full-bodied, with still firm tannins and spicy wood well on the way to integrating and already showing elegance and finesse. Look for layer after layer of currant, blackberry and wild berry fruits, those supported beautifully by notes of cedar, sage and tar, all leading to a near-sweet fruity finish that lingers on and on. Drink now–2016. Score 94.

YARDEN, CABERNET SAUVIGNON, 2004: Dark, almost impenetrable garnet, with generous wood in fine balance with acidity and fruits. Opens to show currants and crushed berries, those yielding to cranberries, ripe purple plums and dark chocolate, all on a background of spices, asphalt and earthiness. Drink now–2016. Score 92.

YARDEN, CABERNET SAUVIGNON, ELROM VINEYARD, 2003: Intensely dark ruby towards royal purple, full-bodied, with caressing tannins and a moderate oak influence. Opens with blackcurrants, blackberries and minerals, goes to meaty, earthy and herbal aromas and flavors, and then to spices and a long and elegant fruity finish. Firmly structured with excellent grip and complexity. Drink now–2020. Score 95.

YARDEN, CABERNET SAUVIGNON, 2003: Aged in French oak for 18 months and showing generous but gentle wood influence. Soft mouth-coating tannins support generous blackberry, black cherry and plum fruits and, on the long finish, hints of Oriental spices and a light herbal-tobacco sensation. Drink now–2014. Score 93.

YARDEN, CABERNET SAUVIGNON, 2002: Dark garnet towards royal purple, full-bodied, with firm tannins and spicy oak yielding nicely to reveal flavors and aromas of red currants, cherries and berries on first attack, those giving way to layers of sweet cedar, vanilla, leather and, on the long finish, a hint of anise. Rich, generous and elegant. Drink now–2012. Score 92.

YARDEN, CABERNET SAUVIGNON, ELROM VINEYARD, 2001: Dark, almost impenetrable garnet-purple, full-bodied, with finely tuned balance between generous well-integrated tannins and judicious oak, this exquisite wine shows complex tiers of aromas and flavors of red currants, berries and spices on the first attack, those opening to include light earthy and herbal overlays. Plush and opulent, with a long, complex finish. Among the best ever made in Israel. Drink now–2013. Score 95.

YARDEN, CABERNET SAUVIGNON, 2001: Full-bodied with finely tuned balance between wood, tannins and fruits. Showing plum, wild berry and spicy currant fruits, and reflecting its 18 months in oak with appealing overlays of vanilla, cedar, tobacco and cocoa. Drink now–2013. Score 91.

YARDEN, MERLOT, 2007: The most full-bodied Yarden Merlot in several years, with gripping but velvety smooth tannins and toasty oak. On first attack ripe raspberries and currants, those making way for light herbal and earthy notes and finally plums and Oriental spices, all culminating in a long mineral-rich finish. Drink now–2015. Score 90.

YARDEN, MERLOT, ODEM VINEYARD, 2006: Made from organically raised grapes. Deep, dark and mysterious, as the wine is still in its prenatal state, but already showing sweet, smoky and spicy oak well matched by mouth-coating tannins. Opens to reveal sweet black cherries, those followed by blackberries and currants and hints of Mediterranean herbs. Drink now–2015. Score 91.

YARDEN, MERLOT, 2006: Inky-dark garnet, medium- to full-bodied with soft tannins, and opening to show mineral, blackberry and raspberry aromas and flavors, those supported by hints of licorice. Drink now–2012. Score 90.

YARDEN, MERLOT, ODEM VINEYARD, 2005: Saturated ruby towards royal purple, full-bodied and intense, this wine was made from organically raised grapes. Opens with an attack of black cherry syrup, that settling down quickly to reveal cherries, berries and cassis along with bitter chocolate and spices. On the long finish gripping tannins rise, together with an appealing hint of licorice. A simultaneously muscular and elegant wine. Drink now–2014. Score 92.

YARDEN, MERLOT, SHA'AL VINEYARD, 2005: Rich and concentrated, a powerhouse at this time waiting for its elements to come together. Already showing fine balance between still gripping tannins and wood with bold aromas and flavors of plum, currant, blackberry, licorice and spices all rising to a long tannic and mineral-rich finish. Drink now–2015. Score 92.

YARDEN, MERLOT, TEL FARAJ VINEYARD, 2005: Full bodied, with caressingly soft tannins and an abundance of blackberry, violet and lightly toasted oak on first attack, those opening to raspberries, mocha and sweet cedar, all building to a long and succulent finish. Drink now–2014. Score 91.

YARDEN, SYRAH, 2007: Still tightly wound and intense but showing good balance and structure that bode well for the future. On the nose and palate almost creamy oak and rich spicy, peppery and meaty overlays on supple blackberries, blueberries and dried currants. Needs time to show its luxurious nature. Best from 2010–2015. Score 90.

YARDEN, SYRAH, 2006: Full-bodied with firm tannins, tangy acidity and spicy wood integrating nicely. Opens to reveal a complex array of plum, currant and berry fruits, those supported nicely by notes of earthy minerals and generously peppered game meat, with tannins and fruits rising comfortably on the long finish. Drink now–2014. Score 90.

YARDEN, SYRAH, 2005: Garnet towards inky-black, full-bodied, with spicy oak and generous soft tannins, showing fine structure and balance. Opens with raspberry and red currant notes, those going on to show generous hints of black pepper, anise and wild berries all coming to a long and generous chocolate and smoky finish. Drink now–2013. Score 91.

YARDEN, SYRAH, ORTAL VINE-YARD, 2004: Perhaps the best Syrah ever in Israel. Extraordinarily deep ruby, full-bodied, with near-sweet tannins integrating nicely with spicy wood. Opens with a burst of almost jammy raspberries and kirsch  liqueur, those yielding to blackberry, cherry and plum fruits. In the background generous hints of anise and Oriental spices and a hint of freshly tanned leather. Drink now–2018. Score 94.

YARDEN, SYRAH, 2004: Medium-dark ruby towards garnet, with firm tannins and spicy oak integrating nicely. Shows a generous array of near jammy raspberries, blackberries, black cherries and plums, those supported by hints of spices, herbs and a hint of polished leather. Drink now–2013. Score 90.

YARDEN, PINOT NOIR, 2007: Medium-bodied, supple, fragrant and graceful, with silky tannins and almost jammy blackberry and currant fruits on a background of white pepper. On the moderately long finish, hints of sandalwood and black cherries. Drink now–2013. Score 90.

YARDEN, PINOT NOIR, 2006: Intense ruby towards garnet, medium- to full-bodied, with well-focused cherry fruits at the core, those opening to reveal plums, dark chocolate and espresso coffee, all leading to a long blackberry-rich finish. Generous, balanced and long, with wood and tannins integrating nicely. Drink now–2013. Score 91.

YARDEN, PINOT NOIR, 2005: The best Pinot Noir yet from the winery. Dark ruby, full-bodied enough to be thought of as fleshy, and with spicy wood and gentle tannins in fine balance with acidity and fruits. Opens with near-sweet, liqueur-like berry aromas and flavors, those yielding in the glass to reveal a crisply dry wine on which you will feel hints of kirsch, dark chocolate and lightly smoked meat, all climaxing in a long and generous blackberry finish. Drink now–2013. Score 93.

YARDEN, PINOT NOIR, 2004: Dark ruby towards garnet, medium- to full-bodied, with well-integrated soft tannins and showing a generous array of blackberry, plum and black cherry fruits, those supported very nicely by hints of pine nuts. On the fruity finish a tantalizing hint of anise. Drink now–2012. Score 90.

YARDEN, CHARDONNAY, ODEM ORGANIC VINEYARD, 2007: Full-bodied, deep golden with a distinct tint of orange that plays in the glass, a wine reflecting generous wood but that in fine proportion to acidity and fruits. Opens with pear, grilled nut and pie crust notes, those going on to show ripe fig, pineapple and baked apple aromas and flavors. Long and creamy with the oak rising on the finish. Drink now–2012. Score 90.

YARDEN, CHARDONNAY, ODEM ORGANIC VINEYARD, 2006: Full-bodied, opening with subtle aromas of figs, pears and apples, going on to show a generous dash of smoky, toasty oak and then blossoming forth with pineapple, citrus peel and minerals leading to a long finish that is simultaneously creamy and bright. Drink now–2013. Score 92.

YARDEN, SAUVIGNON BLANC, 2008: Fresh and lively, damp golden straw in color, medium-bodied, with fine natural acidity to highlight tropical and citrus fruits, those complemented nicely by notes of gooseberries and white pepper. Drink now–2011. Score 89.

YARDEN, VIOGNIER, 2006: Calls to mind the white wines of Condrieu and shows a thoroughly traditional Viognier personality. Following an aromatic and floral nose, flavors and aromas of ripe Anjou pears, peaches, spring flowers and minerals, along with hints of citrus. Lively, clean, fresh and long. Drink now. Score 91.

YARDEN, GEWURZTRAMINER, 2008: The color of freshly dampened straw, showing medium-bodied with traditional Gewurztraminer spices, litchis and floral notes. In the background ripe peaches and a note of citrus peel and finishing with notes of rose petals and minerals. Even though categorized as off-dry, there is but a bare hint of sweetness here, that tantalizing and refreshing. Drink now–2011. Score 90.

Gush Etzion Winery ✶✶✶

GUSH ETZION, CABERNET FRANC, 2005: Dark ruby towards garnet, medium- to full-bodied, with aromas and flavors of tar, bittersweet chocolate and spices overlaying blackberry and blackcurrant fruits. On the long finish, appealing hints of mint. Drink now–2011. Score 89.

Gvaot Winery ✶✶✶

GVAOT, CABERNET SAUVIGNON, HERODION, 2007: Reflecting its 12 months in barriques with gentle spicy oak, this is a medium- to full-bodied red, with soft tannins and a round, fruity personality. On the nose and palate appealing black fruits and a hint of Oriental spices, all lingering nicely, the fruits and tannins rising on a long and mouth-filling finish. Drink now–2011. Score 88.

GVAOT, CABERNET SAUVIGNON, HERODION, 2006: Opens with a lightly funky aroma, that passing quickly. Reflecting its development in barriques with full-body, firm tannins and generous spicy wood, those integrating nicely and showing appealing aromas and flavors of currants, blackberries, green olives and Mediterranean herbs. Drink now–2012. Score 88.

GVAOT, MERLOT, HERODION, 2007: Blended with 10% Cabernet Sauvignon, oak-aged for 12 months, medium- to full-bodied, with soft, caressing tannins and appealing blackcurrant and black cherry fruits, a generous and near-elegant wine with a long licorice-hinted finish. Best 2009–2011. Score 88.

GVAOT, MERLOT, GOFNA RESERVE, 2007: Medium- to full-bodied, opening with an enchanting sawdust and vanilla nose and then going on to show currant and cherry fruits on an earthy and spicy background. A distinctive personality that needs time in the glass to soften. As this develops look for blueberry and chocolate notes. Drink now–2011. Score 89.

GVAOT, MERLOT, RESERVE, 2006: Dark garnet towards royal purple, medium- to full-bodied, with gently mouth-coating tannins. Blended with 10% Cabernet Sauvignon and oak-aged for 14 months, opens to reveal blueberry and black cherry fruits on a background of roasted chestnuts and licorice. Long and generous. Drink now–2011. Score 89.

GVAOT, MERLOT, MASADA, 2006: Dark, almost impenetrable garnet in color, full-bodied, firm and concentrated, opening with peppery cedarwood, that yielding comfortably to blackberry and spicy and earthy aromas and flavors. A distinct personality and a long-lingering finish. Drink now–2012. Score 89.

GVAOT, CABERNET SAUVIGNON-MERLOT, HERODION, 2006: Dark ruby towards garnet, aged for 14 months primarily in used French barriques, this blend of 60% Cabernet Sauvignon and 40% Merlot shows medium-bodied, with gently mouth-coating tannins. Round, soft and rich with appealing red berry and cassis notes, those on a lightly spicy background. Long and generous. Drink now. Score 88.

GVAOT, CABERNET FRANC, GOFNA RESERVE, 2007: As predicted at an early tasting, the best yet from this winery. Medium- to full-bodied, opening with notes of freshly turned earth and loam, those in turn opening to reveal black and blue berries along with spicy and toasty oak notes. Firm tannins but with fine balance and structure, a simultaneously muscular and elegant wine. Drink now–2012. Score 90.

GVAOT, HERODION, BLENDED RED, 2007: A blend of Cabernet Sauvignon, Merlot and Cabernet Franc (60%, 30% and 10% respectively). Oak-aged for 12 months, showing a broad array of black fruits, dark chocolate and tobacco notes on a softly tannic background. Drink now–2011. Score 88.

Hamasrek Winery ✷✷

HAMASREK, CABERNET SAUVIGNON, LIMITED EDITION, SINGLE VINEYARD, JUDEAN HILLS, 2005: Dark royal purple towards garnet in color, full-bodied and reflecting its time in barriques with near-sweet tannins and toasty oak. On the nose and palate red and blackcurrants, raspberries and lightly peppery cedarwood notes, those leading to a long espresso-coffee-rich finish. Drink now. Score 88.

Karmei Yosef Winery (Bravdo) ✷✷✷✷

KARMEI YOSEF, CABERNET SAUVIGNON, BRAVDO, 2007: Full-bodied, with firm, deep tannins and spicy wood, those parting to reveal a core of currant, raspberry, toasty oak and licorice notes. Drink now–2012. Score 88.

KARMEI YOSEF, MERLOT, BRAVDO, 2007: Dark garnet towards royal purple, medium- to full-bodied, with soft, near-sweet tannins and showing a generous array of blackberry, blueberry, spicy and earthy aromas and flavors. Drink now–2011. Score 89.

Katlav Winery ✷✷✷

KATLAV, CABERNET SAUVIGNON, 2007: Dark ruby in color, full-bodied, with near-sweet tannins and light spicy and cedar notes. Opens to reveal a tempting array of blackcurrant, blackberry and purple plum fruits, those complemented by hints of mocha and Mediterranean herbs, all lingering nicely. Drink now–2012. Score 89.

KATLAV, MERLOT, 2007: Dark ruby towards garnet in color, medium-bodied, with soft tannins integrating nicely and showing black cherry, cola and nutmeg on toasty oak, those yielding on the finish to hints of mocha and sage. Deep and long enough to hold our interest. Drink now–2011. Score 89.

Psagot Winery ∗∗∗

PSAGOT, CABERNET SAUVIGNON, 2007: Full-bodied, with firm tannins and smoky wood now integrating nicely and showing rich and generous with well-focused red and blackcurrant fruits overlaid with hints of cocoa and cedarwood. Drink now–2011. Score 88.

PSAGOT, MERLOT, 2006: Dark garnet in color, with generous oak and gripping tannins receding nicely and showing good balance and structure. Fine spices and vanilla here to highlight plum, currant and orange peel notes that go on to a medium-long finish. Drink now. Score 88.

PSAGOT, CABERNET FRANC, 2006: Medium-dark ruby towards garnet in color, medium-bodied, with soft, gently caressing tannins and spicy oak. Showing appealing red currant and raspberry fruits on a background of earthy minerals and herbs and saddle leather. Drink now. Score 88.

PSAGOT, EDOM, 2005: Deep garnet in color, this blend of Cabernet Sauvignon and Merlot (75% and 25% respectively) opens with a rich vanilla and white chocolate nose, then settles down in the glass to reveal aromas and flavors of black cherries, plums and currants. Medium- to full-bodied, with soft but mouth-coating tannins, a good touch of spicy cedarwood and, on the finish, an appealing earthy minerality. Drink now. Score 88.

PSAGOT, VIOGNIER, 2006: Light to medium-bodied, opening with a floral nose and going on to aromas and flavors of summer fruits, green apples and pears, all with a generous mineral note in the background. Drink now. Score 88.

Recanati Winery ✶✶✶✶

Special Reserve Series

SPECIAL RESERVE, 2007: Dark, almost impenetrable garnet in color, full-bodied, with still-gripping tannins starting to settle in nicely and showing fine balance with spicy and lightly smoky wood. Opens with a fruity nose and then goes on to reveal aromas and flavors of currants, cherries and wild berries, those complemented by notes of sweet cedarwood and chocolate. Drink now–2014. Score 90.

SPECIAL RESERVE, 2006: A blend of 97% Cabernet Sauvignon and 3% Merlot. Full-bodied, with firm tannins integrating nicely and showing currant, blackberry and cherry liqueur aromas and flavors. Generous toasty oak here at this stage but that, with the tannins, are settling in nicely to show a simultaneously intense but round and elegant wine. Drink now–2013. Score 90.

SPECIAL RESERVE, 2005: Deep royal purple, full-bodied, with firm, still rough-edged tannins, those integrating nicely with light spicy wood and fruits to show fine balance and structure. A blend of 84% Cabernet Sauvignon and 16% Merlot, this is a big, rich and bold wine, with concentrated layers of currant, blackberry, anise and cedary oak flavors. Drink now–2013. Score 93.

Reserve Series

RESERVE, CABERNET SAUVIGNON, 2006: Dark garnet towards royal purple, medium-to full-bodied (leaning more towards the full), with near-sweet tannins and on the nose and palate a generous array of blackcurrant, blackberry, spice and mocha notes. Juicy and long. Drink now–2011. Score 90.

RESERVE, MERLOT, 2006: Full-bodied, firm in texture, with the tannins just starting to integrate, but already showing forward blackberry and purple plum fruits and developing an appealing hint of mocha. Chewy, round and long. Drink now–2012. Score 90.

RESERVE, MERLOT, 2005: A single vineyard wine, made entirely with grapes from the Manara Vineyard, showing as much as at an earlier tasting. Smooth, round and generous, rich and spicy, with a core of raspberry, cherry and creamy oak backed up by hints of minted chocolate that linger nicely. Good balance between fresh acidity, wood and fruits, and a long finish. Drink now–2011. Score 90.

RESERVE, SYRAH, 2006: Dark garnet in color, with still firm tannins needing time to settle in but showing fine balance and structure. On the nose and palate black cherry and blackcurrant fruits, those matched by hints of grilled beef, herbal and green olive notes. Drink now–2012. Score 89.

RESERVE, SYRAH, 2005: Aged for 14 months in French and American oak. Medium-dark garnet in color, with well-focused tannins and moderate spicy wood in fine balance with black cherry, wild berry and cassis fruits, those with just a hint of smoked meat in the background. Drink now. Score 89.

RESERVE, CABERNET FRANC, 2006: With its once firm tannins now integrating nicely, showing medium-dark garnet, full-bodied, and reflecting its 14 months in oak with generous but not imposing sweet cedar. Dark berry, black cherry and plum fruits highlighted by notes of tobacco, bell peppers and bittersweet chocolate, all lingering nicely on the finish. Drink now–2013. Score 91.

RESERVE, PETITE SIRAH-SHIRAZ, SPECIAL EDITION, 2007: A blend of 60% Petite Sirah and 40% Shiraz, dark royal purple in color, medium-bodied, showing soft, well-integrated tannins and just the right note of dusty oak. On the nose and palate blackberries, blueberries and cassis, those matched nicely by notes of chocolate and mocha. Simultaneously "fun" and elegant. Drink now–2011. Score 90.

RESERVE, PETITE SIRAH-ZINFANDEL, 2006: Reflecting its eight months in oak with gently smoky and spicy wood and softly caressing tannins, a blend of 80% Petite Sirah and 20% Zinfandel. Youthful royal purple, opens to reveal blackberry, pomegranate, mocha and sage notes. Drink now–2012. Score 90.

RESERVE, CHARDONNAY, 2008: An appealing note of spicy oak to show off fine citrus and summer fruits, those with light hints of pepper and juniper berries and, on the generous finish, a tantalizing note of bitter citrus peel. Drink now–2012. Score 89.

Recanati Series

RECANATI, CABERNET SAUVIGNON, 2008: Aging in older barrels and showing a gentle spicy wood influence along with soft, mouth-coating tannins. Opens to reveal red currant, berry and orange peel notes, those supported nicely by notes of freshly cut Mediterranean herbs and earthy minerals. Drink now–2012. Score 90.

RECANATI, CABERNET SAUVIGNON, 2007: Garnet with purple and orange reflections, opens with a rich, fruity nose. Medium- to full-bodied, with soft tannins and a gentle spicy overlay from the wood, and an overall currant and black cherry personality. Smooth, rich and concentrated for the vintage, with tannins rising on the finish. Drink now. Score 89.

RECANATI, MERLOT, 2008: Garnet in color, medium-bodied, with silky, near-sweet tannins. On the nose and palate generous black fruits, cocoa and mocha. Showing soft and round with good grip and length. Drink now–2011. Score 89.

Ruth Winery ✱✱✱

RUTH, CABERNET SAUVIGNON-MERLOT, 2006: A blend of 60% Cabernet Sauvignon and 40% Merlot, developed in oak for 12 months, showing medium- to full-bodied, soft and round with blackberry, currant and black cherry fruits highlighted by notes of bittersweet chocolate and tobacco. Drink now. Score 88.

RUTH, SHIRAZ-MERLOT, 2006: Medium- to full-bodied, a dark garnet blend of equal parts of Shiraz and Merlot, aged in new oak for 15 months. A country-style wine showing generous oak and chunky tannins, but do not take that as negative for the wine opens beautifully on the palate to show red plums and raspberries on a peppery background. Drink now. Score 88.

Sagol (Barry Saslove) ★★★★

SAGOL, CABERNET SAUVIGNON, SINGLE VINEYARD, 2007: Although Barry Saslove's name appears nowhere on this wine, it carries his wine-maker's signature in every way. Oak-aged for six months, and thus reflecting gently spicy wood and soft tannins, this is a soft but concentrated wine showing generous black fruits, those balanced well by hints of spices and tobacco, all coming to a long finish on which you will find notes of dark chocolate and anise creeping comfortably in. Drink now–2012. Score 90.

Segal ★★★★

Unfiltered

UNFILTERED, CABERNET SAUVIGNON, 2005: Blended with 10% Merlot, aged partly in new, partly in used, French and American oak for 30 months, showing full-bodied with generous but gently mouth-coating tannins, the wood and the tannins in fine balance with the fruits. With almost liquor like notes of kirsch and cassis, those yielding comfortably to notes of purple plums and pepper. Long and mouth-filling. Drink now–2011, perhaps longer. Score 91.

UNFILTERED, CABERNET SAUVIGNON, 2004: Blended with 10% of Merlot and oak-aged in French and American barriques for 22 months, showing dark, firm and intense. Full-bodied, with still gripping tannins and generous but not dominating oak, with good balance between those and red and blackcurrants, black cherries, sage and spicy cedarwood on the nose and palate. On the long finish an overlay of minerals and an appealing hint of bitterness. Drink now. Score 90.

Single Vineyard Series

SINGLE VINEYARD, CABERNET SAUVIGNON, DISHON VINEYARD, 2005: Dark, almost inky-garnet in color, concentrated and intense. Full-bodied and tannic enough to be thought of as chewy, the tannins integrating nicely and showing fine balance with the wood in which the wine was aged. Generous black fruits here, but not so much a fruity wine as a spicy one, led by aromas and flavors of smoked bacon, licorice and espresso coffee. Drink now–2012. Score 90.

SINGLE VINEYARD, MERLOT, DOVEV VINEYARD, RECHASIM, 2005: Deeply aromatic, full-bodied with chewy tannins needing time to settle in but showing good balance and structure. Opens to show spicy oak along with black cherry and raspberry fruits, goes on to reveal a tempting herbaceousness and, on the finish, a hint of eucalyptus. Drink now–2011. Score 89.

SINGLE VINEYARD, MERLOT, DOVEV VINEYARD, 2004: Dark garnet towards royal purple, this medium- to full-bodied wine was super-generous with its tannins in its youth, so waiting to release this one was a wise move on the part of the winery. Those tannins are now integrating nicely with spicy cedarwood and showing well-tuned balance and structure. Aromas and flavors of black cherries, blackberries and purple plums, those matched nicely by spicy oak accents and, on the long finish, hints of espresso and dark chocolate. Drink now–2012. Score 90.

"Single" Series

SINGLE, CABERNET SAUVIGNON, MAROM GALIL, 2005: Dark garnet with orange and green reflections, medium- to full-bodied and showing soft tannins, generous oak, and forward blackberry, black cherry and currant fruits on a background of minted chocolate. Generous and long. Drink now. Score 89.

Shiloh ✶✶✶

SHILOH, CABERNET SAUVIGNON, RESERVE, SOD (SECRET), 2006: Developed for 16 months in new and older French barriques, medium- to full-bodied, with soft tannins and notes of sweet cedarwood. An aromatic wine, opening to reveal blackcurrants and black cherries, those matched by notes of citrus peel, chocolate and freshly roasted herbs. Fine balance and a long and generous finish on which the tannins and fruits rise nicely. Drink now–2012. Score 89.

Tabor Winery ✶✶✶✶

Mes'cha

MES'CHA, 2005: Deep, intense and concentrated, full-bodied and with still firm tannins and generous oak waiting to settle down, but showing fine balance and structure that bode well for the future. On the nose and palate currants, wild berries and spices, those supported nicely by light herbal and tobacco notes. Long and generous. Best from 2010–2013. Score 90.

Adama Series

ADAMA, CABERNET SAUVIGNON, BAZELET, 2005: Medium-dark garnet towards purple, this medium- to full-bodied blend of 87% Cabernet Sauvignon and 13% Merlot was developed in 2,000 liter wood casks and shows generous blackcurrant, blackberry, citrus peel and earthy-mineral aromas and flavors. On the long finish, hints of sweet cedar, tobacco and eucalyptus. Drink now–2012. Score 90.

ADAMA, CABERNET SAUVIGNON, BAZELET, 2004: Dark garnet in color, with deep purple and orange reflections, this medium- to full-bodied wine shows good balance between smoky wood, acidity and fruits. On the nose and palate concentrated currant and blackberry fruits matched by espresso and vanilla. Seductive and elegant. Drink now. Score 90.

ADAMA, CABERNET SAUVIGNON, TERRA ROSSA, 2006: Oak-aged for nine months, medium- to full-bodied, with hints of spicy wood and vanilla and gently mouth-coating tannins settling down nicely. Showing currant and blackberry fruits and earthy minerals along with Mediterranean herbs. Round and generous. Drink now–2011. Score 89.

ADAMA, CABERNET SAUVIGNON, TERRA ROSSA, 2005: Dark garnet towards royal purple, medium- to full-bodied, with firm, near-sweet tannins integrating nicely. Aromatic and flavorful, with red plums, raspberries and currants matched by minerals and light hints of herbaceousness. Round, long and generous. Drink now–2011. Score 89.

ADAMA, MERLOT, BAZELET, 2006: Garnet towards royal purple, with light spicy wood and near-sweet tannins and opening to reveal currant, purple plum and blackberry fruits, those on a background of milk chocolate and, on the finish, nice hints of mint and white pepper. Drink now. Score 89.

ADAMA, MERLOT, BAZELET, 2005: Dark ruby towards garnet, medium-bodied and showing red and black berries, red currants, earthy minerals and hints of white chocolate, all on a lightly spicy and herbal background. Blended with 10% of Cabernet Sauvignon, round and generous. Drink now. Score 90.

Tanya Winery***

Enosh Series

ENOSH, CABERNET SAUVIGNON, 2005: The best to date from Tanya. Dark garnet towards royal purple, full-bodied, with soft, gently mouth-coating tannins and spicy wood in fine balance with blackcurrant, blackberry and plum fruits all leading to a long, spicy finish. Drink now. Score 89.

Halal Series

HALAL, CABERNET SAUVIGNON, 2006: Dark garnet towards royal purple, full-bodied, with soft, gently mouth-coating tannins and a moderate hand with spicy wood. Opens to show traditional Cabernet blackcurrant and blackberry fruits, those yielding to show hints of orange peel. Drink now–2011. Score 88.

HALAL, CABERNET SAUVIGNON, 2005: Deep and concentrated, almost impenetrable garnet in color and with firm tannins and generous wood still holding back the fruits here. No fear though, for this one shows fine balance and structure that bode well for the future. Oak-aged for 16 months, opening in the glass to reveal firm but elegant dried currant and blackberry aromas and flavors, those gaining complexity and depth on the long finish. Drink now–2012. Score 90.

HALAL, MERLOT, 2006: Showing even better than at an earlier tasting with Tanya's signature of near-sweet tannins, a soft and generous medium- to full-bodied wine with a plush texture and its cherry, red-berry fruits supported nicely by notes of tobacco, eucalyptus and smoke. Oak-aged for 14 months and with appealing spicy oak notes rising on the finish. Drink now. Score 89.

HALAL, CABERNET FRANC, 2006: Made entirely from Cabernet Franc grapes, developed in barriques for 14 months, dark, almost impenetrable garnet in color, a medium- to full-bodied, softly tannic wine. On first attack notes of plums, tar and bittersweet chocolate, those yielding to aromas and flavors of blackcurrants and espresso coffee, all with a comfortable overlay of black pepper. Long and generous. Drink now–2012. Score 90.

HALAL, CHARDONNAY, 2007: Light, bright golden in color, wisely oaked for only four months, that giving the wine a bare hint of creaminess but not at all hiding the tempting grapefruit, lemon and tropical fruits that make themselves felt nicely. Refreshing and complex enough to grab our attention. Drink now. Score 89.

Teperberg Winery ★★★

Reserve Series

TEPERBERG RESERVE
CABERNET SAUVIGNON
2006

RESERVE, CABERNET SAUVIGNON, 2007: Made entirely from grapes from the Shiloh vineyard, a dark, full-bodied and intense wine with still-deep, almost searing tannins, but already showing balance and structure that bode well for the future. Big and broad-shouldered, with blackberry, blackcurrant, fig and mocha notes backed up by hints of lead pencil and cocoa. Long and generous, an appealing toasty sensation rising on the finish. Drink now–2013. Score 90.

RESERVE, CABERNET SAUVIGNON, 2006: Dark towards inky-garnet, full-bodied, reflecting its 15 months in oak with gentle spices and a bare hint of smoke. Showing still firm tannins, those needing only a bit of time in the glass to settle down and show its fine balance between wood and fruits. On the nose and palate an appealing array of spicy currant, blackberry, cedar and mineral notes, those with a light hint of anise on the long and generous finish. Drink now–2012. Score 89.

RESERVE, MERLOT, 2007: Dark, full-bodied, tannic enough and so packed with currant and blackberry fruits that this one could easily be mistaken for a Cabernet Sauvignon. At this stage a blockbuster, but one that offers the promise of settling down to show an always firm wine, but one that is generous with its fruits (and may well add cherries and raspberries to its repertoire). On the finish, hints of loamy earth and sweet spices. Impressive. Drink now–2013. Score 89.

Terra Series

TEPERBERG
— 1870 —

TERRA

2005

TEPERBERG, CABERNET SAUVIGNON, TERRA, 2005: Dark garnet with purple and orange reflections, this wine shows a gentle hand with spicy oak and soft tannins. On the nose and palate traditional Cabernet blackcurrant and blackberry fruits, those with spice and orange peel overlays and, on the moderately long finish, an appealing hint of cigar tobacco. Drink now. Score 90.

TEPERBERG, MERLOT, TERRA, 2006: Garnet towards royal purple, medium-bodied, with caressing tannins, reflecting its 12 months in oak with gentle spices and smoke. On the nose and palate currant, blackberry and cranberry fruits, those backed up nicely by a light earthy-herbal overlay. Drink now. Score 88.

TEPERBERG, MALBEC, TERRA, 2007: Nicely focused, with black cherry, currant and cocoa notes along with hints of sweet toast and vanilla. Medium-bodied, with soft tannins, most assuredly not an Argentinean Malbec but a very pleasant Mediterranean version. Drink now. Score 88.

Tishbi Winery ✳✳✳

Special Reserve Series

SPECIAL RESERVE, 2004: Super-dark garnet in color, full-bodied, a blend of 50% Cabernet Sauvignon, 40% Merlot and 10% Cabernet Franc, the grapes from Sde Boker in the Negev. Good balance between firm tannins, spicy wood and fruits, showing appealing blackcurrant, blackberry and tobacco notes. On the long finish a light minty note. Drink now. Score 90.

SPECIAL RESERVE, CABERNET SAUVIGNON-MERLOT-CABERNET FRANC, 2004: Dark garnet, medium- to full-bodied, this oak-aged blend of 50% Cabernet Sauvignon, 40% Merlot and 10% Cabernet Franc was made entirely from grapes harvested at Sde Boker in the Negev. Good balance between still firm tannins, spicy wood and black fruits, those matched by tobacco and chocolate and a long, lightly minty finish. Drink now. Score 90.

Estate Series

ESTATE, CABERNET SAUVIGNON, 2005: Deep garnet with violet and orange reflections, medium- to full-bodied, with still firm tannins but those in fine balance with acidity, wood and fruits. A blend of 90% Cabernet Sauvignon, 7% Cabernet Franc and 3% Petit Verdot, oak-aged for about 13 months, showing an appealing layer of spiciness together with currant and blackberry fruits. Drink now–2011. Score 90.

ESTATE, SHIRAZ, 2005: Dark cherry towards garnet in color, medium- to full-bodied, with soft tannins integrating nicely. On the nose and palate cherry, raspberry and spicy aromas and flavors on a light earthy background. Drink now. Score 89.

ESTATE, CABERNET FRANC, 2006: Showing much as at an earlier tasting. Dark garnet in color, full-bodied and with chewy tannins, a well-focused wine, its spicy (almost peppery) wood settling down nicely to show a fine array of currant and blackberry fruits, those with an appealing leathery overtone. Long and satisfying. Best 2009–2012. Score 89.

Tzora Vineyards ∗∗∗∗

Misty Hills

TZORA VINEYARDS, MISTY HILLS, 2006: A blend of equal parts of Cabernet Sauvignon and Syrah, those aged for 18 months in barriques. Deep and youthful royal purple in color, full-bodied, concentrated and intense, showing generous mouth-coating tannins and a judicious hand with the oak, all in fine balance with fruits. On first attack strawberries and red currants, those going to black fruits on a background of earthy minerals and Oriental spices. As this one continues to develop, look as well for notes of saddle leather and tobacco. Drink now–2015. Score 92.

Tzora Vineyards Series

TZORA VINEYARDS, CABERNET SAUVIGNON, GIVAT HACHALUKIM, 2007: Dark garnet in color, generously aromatic, a medium- to full-bodied red with soft tannins integrating nicely with spicy wood and fruits. On the nose and palate opening with raspberries, those going to blackberries, currants and hints of orange peel. Firm but yielding, generous and long. Drink now–2012. Score 90.

TZORA VINEYARDS, CABERNET SAUVIGNON, GIVAT HACHALUKIM, 2006: Made entirely from Cabernet Sauvignon grapes, with softly caressing tannins and reflecting a gentle hand with oak. Medium- to full-bodied, with generous currant and wild berry fruits, those matched nicely by hints of anise and white pepper. Finishes moderately long with a note of minted chocolate. Drink now. Score 88.

TZORA VINEYARDS, CABERNET SAUVIGNON, NEVE ILAN, 2006: Medium- to full-bodied, this deep garnet-towards-royal purple wine's firm tannins are integrating with wood and fruits. Showing generous raspberry and red currant and a youthful cranberry hint, with the tannins coating the mouth nicely. Opening to reveal earthy minerals, and, on the long finish, gentle hints of spicy wood and freshly picked mushrooms. Drink now–2011. Score 89.

TZORA VINEYARDS, CABERNET SAUVIGNON, SHORESH, 2006: Dark royal purple, with appealingly herbal and earthy notes. Medium- to full-bodied, showing generous cherry, berry and cassis fruits, those finishing with hints of coffee and tobacco. Drink now. Score 89.

TZORA VINEYARDS, CABERNET SAUVIGNON, GIVAT HACHALUKIM, 2005: Dark ruby towards garnet, medium- to full-bodied, with soft tannins and generous spicy wood. Opens to show generous red and black fruits, those supported nicely by hints of freshly turned earth and tobacco. Drink now. Score 90.

TZORA VINEYARDS, MERLOT, NEVE ILAN, 2006: Garnet-red with orange and purple reflections, this medium- to full-bodied wine shows generous but near-sweet soft tannins integrating nicely, and already opening to reveal bountiful red fruits and an appealing spicy overlay. Tannins and steely minerals rise pleasantly on the finish to make this a very fine Merlot. Drink now–2011. Score 89.

TZORA VINEYARDS, MERLOT, SHORESH, 2005: Dark garnet towards royal purple, medium- to full-bodied, with soft, mouth-coating tannins and spicy wood integrating nicely. Opens to show a fine array of berry, black cherry and citrus peel, those leading to a moderately long finish. Drink now. Score 89.

TZORA VINEYARDS, CABERNET SAUVIGNON-MERLOT, NEVE ILAN, 2007: Dark garnet towards royal purple, medium- to full-bodied (perhaps destined in the end to be full-bodied) with generous mouth-coating tannins and spicy wood in fine balance with red currant and wild berry fruits, those on a background that hints nicely of tobacco and freshly turned soil. Rich and firm but with the clear promise for elegance. Drink now–2013. Score 90.

TZORA VINEYARDS, CABERNET SAUVIGNON-SYRAH, SHORESH, 2007: Dark, almost inky-garnet in color, full-bodied, with firm, still-gripping but near-sweet tannins needing time to integrate, but already promising fine balance and structure. Opens with blackcurrants and purple plums, those coming together nicely with grilled herbs, cigar tobacco and, on the long finish, appealing hints of saddle leather and bitter orange peel. Drink now–2013. Score 89.

TZORA VINEYARDS, SYRAH-CABERNET SAUVIGNON, MEUBANIM, 2006: Meubanim is a sub-section of the Shoresh vineyard, an area of particularly low yield and judged to be individual enough in personality that the grapes were separated for this special blend. Full-bodied, with firm, almost puckering tannins and leathery and gamey on the nose, but showing promise for integration and a muscular kind of elegance. Opens to reveal red currants, raspberries, chocolate and tobacco. Long, intense and mouth-filling. Drink now–2011. Score 90.

TZORA VINEYARDS, GEWURZTRAMINER, SHORESH BLANC, 2007: Bright golden in color, opening on the nose with what seem like sweet fruits but comes to the palate as completely dry, showing litchi, kiwi and peach fruits. Medium-bodied, soft, round and caressing, and ends with a light honeyed note that lingers nicely. Drink now. Score 88.

Tzuba Winery ✱✱✱

Hametzuda Series

HAMETZUDA, 2006: Made entirely from Cabernet Sauvignon grapes, deep purple, medium- to full-bodied, with generous soft tannins coming together with notes of spicy wood, and opening to show currants and red and black berries. As the wine develops look as well for notes of espresso coffee and green olives. Long and generous. Drink now–2012. Score 88.

HAMETZUDA, 2005: A blend of 75% Merlot and 25% Cabernet Sauvignon, oak-aged for 24 months. Medium-dark garnet, full-bodied, with near-sweet tannins now integrating nicely to show an appealing array of blackberry, cherry and herbal notes. A gentle spicy wood influence and a hint of licorice on the long finish add to the charms of the wine. Drink now. Score 88.

HAMETZUDA, CHARDONNAY, 2007: Oaked for only three and a half months, this medium-bodied, light gold wine shows a light green tint and opens to reveal generous summer and tropical fruits on a background of lively acidity. On the finish an appealing hint of green apples. Drink now. Score 88.

Tel Tzuba Series

TEL TZUBA, CABERNET SAUVIGNON, 2007: Medium- to full-bodied, with softly caressing tannins. Dark garnet towards royal purple, opening with red berries, those yielding comfortably to currants and blueberries on a gently spicy background. Fruits and tannins rise on the finish. Drink now–2011. Score 88.

TEL TZUBA, CABERNET SAUVIGNON, 2006: Reflecting spices and near-sweet tannins from its 14 months in French oak, a medium- to full-bodied red with good concentration, soft tannins and a gentle wood influence. On the nose and palate starts off with blackcurrants and blackberries, those yielding to a pleasing red berry-cherry character and finally, on the long finish, notes of Mediterranean herbs. Drink now–2011. Score 90.

TEL TZUBA, MERLOT, 2007: Extraordinarily dark and concentrated yet simultaneously round and elegant. Generously aromatic, full-bodied, firmly tannic and intense, but even at this early stage showing fine balance and structure. On the nose and palate juicy blueberry, raspberry and white pepper, all lingering nicely on a smooth, coffee-scented finish. Drink now–2012. Score 90.

TEL TZUBA, SHIRAZ, 2007: Dark garnet towards royal purple, medium- to full-bodied, with generous but not overpowering spicy oak and vanilla, those parting to reveal raspberry, cherry and red plum fruits in fine harmony with spices and notes of leather. Potentially polished, long and well focused. Drink now–2013. Score 90.

TEL TZUBA, SHIRAZ, 2006: Garnet towards royal purple, medium- to full-bodied, with good concentration and balance. Firm tannins are settling in nicely now and part to reveal cherry, blueberry and cassis notes, those with hints of spices and saddle leather. Drink now–2012. Score 89.

TEL TZUBA, PINOT NOIR, 2007: Pinot with a distinctly Burgundian flavor. Dark ruby in color, medium- to full-bodied, with generously caressing soft tannins. On first attack quite firm, but opens in the glass to show first floral, mineral and raspberry fruits and then black cherries, green tea and notes of both Oriental spices and saddle leather. Drink now–2012. Score 88.

TEL TZUBA, SANGIOVESE, 2007: Medium-bodied, pale garnet in color and with soft tannins and showing a generous array of berry, black cherry and strawberry fruits. Soft and round, reflecting its 14 months in French oak with light toasty overtones. Drink now. Score 88.

TEL TZUBA, SANGIOVESE, 2006: A blend of 85% Sangiovese and 15% Nebbiolo, oak-aged for 14 months, showing medium- to full-bodied, with soft tannins integrating nicely. Generous raspberry and cherry fruits on first attack open to show blueberries and notes of spices. Round, soft and complex, although easy to drink. Drink now. Score 89.

Yatir Winery *****

Yatir Forest

YATIR FOREST, 2006: Dark garnet in color, with orange and green reflections, full-bodied and showing soft, mouth-coating tannins and a moderate touch of spicy oak. A Bordeaux blend, opening to show tempting currant, blackberry and black cherry fruits, those on a background of exotic spices and an enchanting hint of bitter chocolate that comes in on the finish. Drink now–2014. Score 91.

YATIR FOREST, 2005: A full-bodied Bordeaux blend of 77% Cabernet Sauvignon, 13% Petit Verdot and 10% Merlot. A third aged in new and two-thirds aged in old wood barriques for 15 months, this deep royal purple wine casts intense orange and green reflections. Soft tannins integrating beautifully and, with the intentionally gentle hand with the wood, come together nicely to let the wine open with spicy berry and cassis aromas and flavors, those going on to show blackberries and an underlying and fascinating mélange of bitter herbs. Long, generous and elegant. Drink now–2014. Score 94.

YATIR FOREST, 2004: Almost inky in its deep garnet color, this full-bodied blend of Cabernet Sauvignon, Merlot and Syrah (80%, 14% and 6% respectively) is showing elegant and solid, with soft tannins, smoky wood and vanilla, all in fine balance with ripe blueberry, blackcurrant, and plum flavors. Look as well for an appealing, earthy undercurrent leading to a long, deep, broad and generous finish. Drink now–2014. Score 93.

Yatir Series

YATIR, CABERNET SAUVIGNON, 2006: Rich and deeply extracted, with generous blackberry, currant, black cherry and wild berries that are highlighted by mocha, vanilla and cedarwood overtones. Destined for elegance. Drink now–2015. Score 93.

YATIR, CABERNET SAUVIGNON, 2005: Blended with 15% of Shiraz, this dark garnet with purple and orange reflections is showing fine balance between gentle spicy wood and mouth-coating tannins that are integrating nicely. On first attack blackberries and currants, those yielding to raspberries, spices and light overlays of earthiness and leather, all with a hint of what at one moment feels like lead pencil and the next like cigar box. Long, generous and destined for elegance. Drink now–2014. Score 92.

YATIR, MERLOT, 2006: Dark and dense but even at this early stage showing admirable depth, length and complexity. On the nose and palate layer after layer of currants, black cherries, chocolate and mocha all backed up by tannins that are simultaneously soft and powerful. Drink now–2014. Score 92.

YATIR, MERLOT, 2005: Medium- to full-bodied, with generous near-sweet tannins, this seductive wine is already showing delicious blueberry, blackberry, mocha and vanilla flavors. Plush and round, on the way to becoming a delicious, complex and concentrated wine. Drink now–2012. Score 90.

YATIR, SHIRAZ, 2006: Full-bodied and concentrated with still firm tannins that need time to settle in. Showing fine balance and structure, the tannins integrating nicely now with a gentle spicy wood influence and opening in the glass to show blackberry, black cherry and prune notes, those on a background that hints of grilled beef and dark chocolate. Drink now–2017. Score 93.

YATIR, SHIRAZ, 2005: Dark, almost impenetrable garnet in color, intentionally aged in old oak barriques in order to highlight the typical characteristics of the variety but still showing generous wood, the wine opens with meaty and herbal aromas, those yielding nicely to cherry, red currant and berry fruits and finally, creeping in comfortably, an agreeable hint of saddle leather. Long, generous and destined for intense elegance. Drink now–2014. Score 93.

YATIR, CABERNET FRANC, 2006: Deep royal purple, full-bodied, and showing faithful to the variety with complex black cherry, blackberry and cassis fruits accented by spices, cedarwood, coffee and hints of tar and vanilla. Drink now–2011. Score 90.

YATIR, PETIT VERDOT, 2006: Deep purple, a powerful wine with intense tannins, concentration and complexity. On the nose and palate layers of plum, blackberry, pomegranate, coffee and earth, those already showing hints of smoky oak. An outstanding example of a variety that is not often bottled on its own. Drink now–2013. Score 92.

YATIR, BLENDED RED, 2005: A blend of Merlot, Shiraz, Cabernet Franc and Petit Verdot (37%, 36%, 15% and 12% respectively). Aged in oak for 12 months, this still-young wine shows firm tannins nicely balanced with lightly spicy wood. Starts with a rich blackberry nose and then goes on to aromas and flavors of wild berries, currants and anise, all on a gently herbal background. Drink now–2012. Score 90.

YATIR, SAUVIGNON BLANC, 2007: Showing elegance and subtlety with citrus, passion fruit, green apple and grapefruit aromas and flavors on a grassy and stony-mineral background. Well crafted. Drink now. Score 90.

YATIR, VIOGNIER, 2007: Light golden straw in color, made entirely from Viognier grapes, some intentionally harvested early, some quite late and wisely unoaked to maintain the fruity and aromatic nature of the variety. Rich, ripe and crispy dry, a generous mouthful of pear, green apple, melon and summer fruits, those backed up by crisp acidity and a hint of unsweetened cream on the long finish. Drink now–2011. Score 92.

Zion Winery ✳✳✳

ZION, ARMON, 2005: Aged partly in new and partly in one- and two-year-old American barriques for 24 months, a medium- to full-bodied blend of 65% Cabernet Sauvignon, 30% Merlot and 5% Petite Sirah. On the nose and palate generous currant, blackberry and purple plum fruits, those supported nicely by notes of spices, espresso coffee and earthy minerals. Drink now–2011. Score 90.

THE UNITED STATES

California

Covenant Winery ✳✳✳✳✳

Covenant

COVENANT, CABERNET SAUVIGNON, NAPA VALLEY, 2008: Impenetrably dark garnet in color, made from 20-year-old low-yield vines, opens with dusty wood and near-sweet tannins that coat the mouth gently, those yielding to generous black fruits and notes of both dark chocolate and licorice, with the fruits rising on the long and mouth-filling finish. Best 2011–2018. Tentative 92.

COVENANT, CABERNET SAUVIGNON, NAPA VALLEY, 2006: Every bit as excellent as earlier releases, but perhaps destined to be the longest-lived of the Covenant wines released to date. Dark garnet towards royal purple, full-bodied, with silky smooth, near-sweet tannins that caress gently and showing fine balance between those, a bare hint of smoky wood, and fruits. On the nose and palate ripe currants and plums, those matched nicely by notes of basil, and then followed with notes of chocolate. Drink now–2018. Score 94.

COVENANT, CABERNET SAUVIGNON, NAPA VALLEY, 2005: Dark garnet with orange and green reflections, full-bodied, with soft, caressing tannins and showing fine balance and structure that bode well for the future. On the nose and palate opens with ripe plums and a hint of licorice, those yielding nicely to blackcurrants, Oriental spices and, on the long finish, a hint of cigar tobacco. Drink now–2017. Score 92.

COVENANT, CABERNET SAUVIGNON, NAPA VALLEY, 2004: Dark ruby towards garnet, full-bodied, with soft tannins integrating nicely and fine balance between those, toasty wood and fruits. On the nose and palate a tempting array of red currants and red and black berries, those complemented nicely by hints of tobacco and herbs and, on the moderately long finish, a pleasant hint of earthiness. Drink now–2012. Score 90.

COVENANT, CABERNET SAUVIGNON, NAPA VALLEY, 2003: Dark ruby towards royal purple, medium- to full-bodied, with generous but soft tannins integrating nicely and gentle overlays of vanilla and spices from aging in new French barriques. Near-sweet blackcurrant aromas and flavors abound, those matched nicely by hints of berries, tobacco and Mediterranean herbs. Long, round and mouth-filling. Drink now–2013. Score 93.

COVENANT, CHARDONNAY, WHITE COVENANT, RUSSIAN RIVER, SONOMA, 2008: Deep gold, a big wine just starting on its way but already showing a distinctive personality. Opens with pears, figs and anise, goes on to peaches and honeysuckle and finally, on the long finish, a note of licorice. Long and complex, far from your standard Chardonnay and well worth trying. Best 2010–2015. Score 90.

Red C

COVENANT, RED C, NAPA VALLEY, 2008: Dark garnet towards royal purple in color, medium- to full-bodied, with soft tannins and gentle wood influences. On the nose and palate blackcurrants, blackberries and black cherries, those matched nicely by notes of bittersweet chocolate, *garrigue* and roasted herbs. Best 2011–2016. Tentative Score 89–91.

COVENANT, RED C, NAPA VALLEY, 2006: Call this the second wine of Covenant if you will but a wine that stands comfortably on its own and, as a second wine should do, offers an early preview of what is to come in the future. Garnet towards royal purple, medium- to full-bodied, a Cabernet Sauvignon blend showing silky tannins and gentle spicy wood influences. Opens to reveal currants and red and black berries on a background of mocha and an intriguing note of stony minerals that comes in on the long finish. Drink now–2013. Score 90.

COVENANT, RED C, NAPA VALLEY, 2005: Dark ruby towards garnet, medium- to full-bodied, with soft, gently mouth-coating tannins and a light hand with the oak in which it was developed. Opens to show traditional Cabernet Sauvignon aromas and flavors of blackcurrants and blackberries, those coming together nicely with hints of orange peel and Mediterranean herbs. I am well aware that sunshine has neither aroma nor flavor, but so help me, this one tastes of sunshine. Drink now–2011. Score 89.

Four Gates Winery★★★★

FOUR GATES, CABERNET SAUVIGNON, SANTA CRUZ MOUNTAINS, 2005: Garnet to royal purple, with firm, drying tannins but with good balance and focus. On the nose and palate blackcurrant, black cherry and blackberry fruits, those supported by hints of Oriental spices. Concentrated and long. Drink now–2012. Score 89.

FOUR GATES, MERLOT, LA ROCHELLE, SANTA CRUZ MOUNTAINS, 2007: Dark garnet, showing generous spicy oak and firm tannins from its 24 months in barriques. Full-bodied and muscular, opening slowly in the glass to reveal deep layers of blueberries, currants and dark chocolate. Drink now–2013. Score 89.

FOUR GATES, MERLOT, SANTA CRUZ MOUNTAINS, 2006: A blockbuster Merlot, developed in oak for 24 months with 15.3% alcohol, firm but smooth tannins and a sweet hint from the alcohol. On the nose and palate currants and blueberries, those complemented by notes of earthy minerals and roasted herbs. Drink now–2013. Score 90.

FOUR GATES, MERLOT, M.S.C., SANTA CRUZ MOUNTAINS, 2005: Well structured, with currant, berry and mineral aromas and flavors coming together nicely with firm but ripe tannins and cedarwood. On the finish, hints of spices and salted roasted nuts. Give this one some time in the glass to reveal its charms. Drink now–2012. Score 89.

FOUR GATES, SYRAH, SANTA CRUZ MOUNTAINS, 2005: Super-dark garnet in color, full-bodied, with generous tannins and wood, those in fine balance with fruits and natural acidity. On the nose and palate sweet spices and a hint of leather to highlight jammy raspberries, wild berries and purple plums. Fruit-forward enough that many will feel a hint of sweetness here. Long and mouth-filling. Drink now–2012. Score 90.

FOUR GATES, SYRAH, SANTA CRUZ MOUNTAINS, 2004: Deep, almost impenetrable garnet, full-bodied, with firm tannins and notes of smoke and spices from the barriques in which it aged, those well balanced by generous blackberry, black cherry, mocha and peppery notes. On the long finish a hint of saddle leather. Drink now–2011. Score 89.

FOUR GATES, SYRAH, SPECIAL RESERVE, WEBB FAMILY VINEYARD, SANTA CLARA VALLEY, 2003: Almost inky-dark royal purple in color, full-bodied, with mouth-coating tannins and generous sweet spices running through, those never quite yielding but sharing the spotlight with wild berries, sur-ripe plums and equally generous wood. Along with all of this, a sensation of sweet raspberry confiture that runs through from first attack to the long finish. Drink now–2013, perhaps longer. Score 91.

FOUR GATES, CABERNET FRANC, SANTA CRUZ MOUNTAINS, 2006: Deep, almost impenetrable garnet, full-bodied, with gently mouth-coating tannins. Opens with traditional Cabernet Franc green notes on the nose, those melding together with cherry, raspberry and rose petal notes, all coming together in a silky and generous wine. Drink now–2013. Score 90.

FOUR GATES, CABERNET FRANC, SANTA CRUZ MOUNTAINS, 2005: Medium-bodied, dark ruby towards garnet in color, with moderately firm tannins integrating nicely to show dried cherry, red currant and *garrigue*, all coming together nicely. Long and mouth-filling. Drink now. Score 87.

FOUR GATES, CHARDONNAY, SANTA CRUZ MOUNTAINS, 2007: Fermented on its lees in barriques for 12 months, a buttery yet crisp white, showing citrus, mango and kiwi fruits supported by light spices and minerals. Drink now. Score 89.

FOUR GATES, CHARDONNAY, SANTA CRUZ MOUNTAINS, 2005: Generously oaked and showing spicy cedar and buttery notes, those opening to melon, pear and mango notes. Long, generous and mouth-filling. Drink now. Score 89.

Hagafen Winery ★★★★★

Prix Reserve Series

HAGAFEN, PRIX MÉLANGE, NAPA VALLEY, 2005: Perhaps not the magnificent 2004 wine but superb in its own right, calling far more to mind the wines of Bordeaux's right bank than those of California. Full-bodied, with gently mouth-coating tannins, opens with red and black berries, those yielding to currants, violets, chocolate and peppery notes. On the long finish, tempting hints of cinnamon and white chocolate. Drink now–2014. Score 93.

HAGAFEN, PRIX MÉLANGE, NAPA VALLEY, 2004: Very possibly the best ever from Ernie Weir at Hagafen and one of the best kosher wines ever. A Bordeaux blend, medium- to full-bodied, with soft tannins, gently vanilla-rich wood, and acidity and fruits in fine balance. On first attack generous cherry, red berry and cassis, those yielding to blackberries and spring flowers and then chocolate, white pepper and cinnamon, all of which come together harmoniously and linger on and on in a mouth-filling finish. Drink now–2015. Score 95.

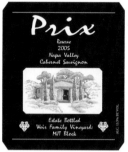

HAGAFEN, CABERNET SAUVIGNON, PRIX RESERVE, WEIR FAMILY VINEYARD, MJT BLOCK, NAPA VALLEY, 2005: As the song has it, black is the color of my true love's hair, and so it is with this wine. Almost impenetrably black in color, full-bodied, with firm tannins and generous wood waiting to integrate, opens slowly in the glass to reveal blackcurrant, blackberry and black cherry fruits, those on a background of earthy minerals. Look as well for hints of eucalyptus and green olives on the long finish. Best from 2010–2016, perhaps longer. Score 93.

HAGAFEN, CABERNET SAUVIGNON, PRIX RESERVE, WEIR FAMILY VINEYARD, MJT BLOCK, NAPA VALLEY, 2004: Like the 2002 and 2003 editions of this wine that I tasted earlier, a true blockbuster Cabernet. Deep garnet in color, full-bodied, with still gripping tannins just starting to settle in, but showing fine balance and structure. On the nose and palate forward blackberry, blackcurrant and purple plum fruits, those supported nicely by generous hints of spices, roasted herbs and a note of cigar tobacco that comes in on the long, long finish. Drink now–2015, perhaps longer. Score 92.

HAGAFEN, CABERNET SAUVIGNON, PRIX RESERVE, MJT BLOCK, NAPA VALLEY, 2003: Dark garnet towards black, blended with 12% of Cabernet Franc, full-bodied, and with soft, gently mouth-coating tannins yielding nicely to spicy wood and opening to reveal an array of blackcurrant, black cherry and bittersweet chocolate, all on a background of licorice and minerals. On the long finish tannins and red berries rise to add to the complexity of the wine. Drink now–2013, perhaps longer. Score 92.

HAGAFEN, MERLOT, PRIX RESERVE, VICHY VINEYARD, BLOCK 4, NAPA VALLEY, 2006: Deep, dark and mysterious, well focused and complex. Full-bodied, with gently mouth-coating tannins and just the right notes of spicy and vanilla-rich wood, those in fine balance with black cherry, currant, herbal and spicy flavors. A long finish here, on which the tannins and fruits rise together. Drink now–2014. Score 93.

HAGAFEN, MERLOT, PRIX RESERVE, VICHY VINEYARD, BLOCK 4, NAPA VALLEY, 2005: Full-bodied, with soft tannins and a moderate hand with the oak. Opens to show black and red cherries, goes on to reveal blueberries and hints of pepper and cigar tobacco. Drink now–2011. Score 91.

HAGAFEN, PINOT NOIR, PRIX RE-SERVE. SOLEIL VINEYARD, NORTH BLOCK, NAPA VALLEY, 2006: Medium- to full-bodied, with gripping, mouth-coating tannins. Dark cherry red, opens with a burst of red cherries, raspberries and cassis, those on a background of Oriental spices and white pepper. Intriguing. Drink now–2014. Score 92.

HAGAFEN, SYRAH, PRIX RESERVE, NAPA VALLEY-SONOMA, 2005: Dark garnet in color, medium- to full-bodied, with fine balance between lightly smoky wood, gentle tannins and fruits. On the opening nose a generous hint of cherries, that gliding gently into aromas and flavors of raspberries, strawberries and red currants, all matched comfortably by notes of cigar tobacco and baker's chocolate. On the long finish-hints of black pepper and saddle leather. Well crafted. Drink now–2012, perhaps longer. Score 92.

HAGAFEN, PINOT NOIR, PRIX RESERVE, FAGEN CREEK VINE-YARD, BLOCK 38, NAPA VALLEY, 2006: Dark cherry-red towards garnet, medium- to full-bodied, with gently mouth-coating tannins. A well-balanced and structured red, opening in the glass to reveal an unusual but tempting set of aromas and flavors for Pinot, those including smoked meat, espresso coffee and black licorice, the major fruity component being of cherries. On the long finish, notes of cloves and nutmeg. You may love it or you may not but it will surely tantalize. Drink now–2015. Score 91.

HAGAFEN, ZINFANDEL, PRIX RESERVE, MOSCOWITE RANCH, BLOCK 61, NAPA VALLEY, 2006: Dark and brooding, showing full-bodied and firmly tannic at this stage but with fine balance and structure that bode well for the future. Plenty of *garrigue* here but over that generous black fruits, dark chocolate, espresso coffee and, on the long finish a hint of vanilla pudding. Approachable now, but best 2011–2015. Score 92.

HAGAFEN, WHITE RIESLING, PRIX RESERVE, RANCHO WIERU-ZOWSKI VINEYARD, NAPA VALLEY, 2007: Gold towards orange in color, with an appealing oily-petrol texture and generous minerals in the background. Opens to reveal generous honeyed apricots, sugar-glazed citrus peel and distinct notes of key lime pie. Long and generous, an idiosyncratic but lovely wine, its generous sweetness set off nicely by finely tuned acidity. This one will cellar nicely. Approachable and enjoyable now but best 2011–2018. Score 93.

HAGAFEN, CHARDONNAY, PRIX RESERVE, HALL VINEYARD, "D" BLOCK, OAK KNOLL DISTRICT, NAPA VALLEY, 2006: Gold with orange tints, full-bodied and generously enough oaked to be thought of as creamy and buttery. On first attack cedarwood and caramelized fruits, those parting to make way for summer fruits, green apples and a note of white raisins. Long, powerful and well crafted—but primarily for those who enjoy their whites with a heavy dose of oak. Drink now–2015. Score 91.

Hagafen Series

HAGAFEN, CABERNET SAUVIGNON, NAPA VALLEY, 2006: Almost impenetrably dark garnet in color, full-bodied, with still gripping tannins waiting to settle down. Opens in the glass to reveal currant, blackberry and black cherry fruits, those complemented nicely by notes of tobacco, espresso coffee and bitter-sweet chocolate. Approachable and enjoyable now, but best from 2011–2015. Score 90.

HAGAFEN, CABERNET SAUVIGNON, NAPA VALLEY, 2004: Blended with 10% Cabernet Franc, oak aged for 19 months, almost penetrable garnet in color, full-bodied, deep and concentrated, with firm tannins and peppery oak integrating nicely. On first attack black cherries and purple plums, those yielding to red currants and notes of bitter-sweet chocolate. Long and generous. Drink now–2014. Score

HAGAFEN, CABERNET SAUVIGNON NAPA VALLEY, 2003: Dark garnet, full-bodied with firm tannins and generous near-sweet cedar-wood, the wine opens in the glass to reveal blackberries, currants and citrus peel. A long finish on which one finds notes of chocolate and tobacco. Drink now–2012, perhaps longer. Score 89.

HAGAFEN, MERLOT, NAPA VALLEY, 2006: A medium- to full-bodied, softly tannic, fruit-driven Merlot that surprises by its unusual array of aromas and flavors, those including black cherries, blackberries and red licorice, all accompanied by notes of nutmeg, cinnamon and citrus peel. Unusual but delicious. Drink now–2011. Score 90.

HAGAFEN, MERLOT, NAPA VALLEY, 2005: Medium-dark garnet in color, medium- to full-bodied, with soft, gently mouth-coating tannins and concentrated fruits. Opens with an appealing note of freshly turned earth, that going on to spicy, almost chili-pepper-scented blackberry, currant and plum fruits. Softens and turns gentle and elegant on the long finish. Drink now–2012. Score 90.

HAGAFEN, SYRAH, NAPA VALLEY, 2003: The fourth time I have tasted this wine and still no reason to take back all of the good things I have said about it in the past. With its chocolate-covered cherry flavors and generous spicy oak, this wine calls out California in a big way, but with its firm tannins, spicy oak, tobacco, and leathery and meaty overlays, it calls out the Rhone Valley no less. Whatever, a lovely wine—dark garnet with green and purple reflections, full-bodied and with its firm tannins now integrating nicely. On the nose and palate generous black cherry and cassis fruits, those matched nicely by earthy minerals, chocolate and a tempting herbal overlay. Long, concentrated and intense. Give this one some time to show its elegance. Drink now–2012. Score 90.

HAGAFEN, PINOT NOIR, NAPA VALLEY, 2007: Medium-dark cherry in color, medium-bodied, with soft, well-integrating tannins and a silky mouth-feel. On the nose and palate near-jammy strawberries and black cherries, those enhanced by notes of espresso coffee and bittersweet chocolate. Lingers nicely. Drink now–2014. Score 89.

HAGAFEN, PINOT NOIR, NAPA VALLEY, 2006: Cherry red towards garnet in color, floral on the nose, a stylish and supple wine, showing a generous array of cherry, pomegranate and red currant fruits, those on a background of green tea and vanilla. Soft tannins linger on a finish of minerals, pepper and cedarwood. Drink now–2012. Score 90.

HAGAFEN, ZINFANDEL, NAPA VALLEY, 2005: A well-focused wine, medium-bodied, with soft, gently mouth-coating tannins and just the barest tantalizing hints of spicy oak. Opens with black cherry and sage notes, those going on to reveal ripe plum, licorice and mineral notes. Long and generous. Drink now–2011. Score 90.

HAGAFEN, CHARDONNAY, OAK KNOLL, NAPA VALLEY, 2006: Golden straw in color, this medium- to full-bodied white shows tantalizing hints of toasty and spicy oak. Opens with citrus and apple aromas and flavors, those on a lightly creamy background, and then going on to reveal notes of ripe peaches and citrus peel. A white that will go as well with fish, chicken or veal. Drink now. Score 90.

HAGAFEN, SAUVIGNON BLANC, 30TH AN-NIVERSARY, NAPA VALLEY, 2008: Light gold in color, medium-bodied and unoaked, with crisp acidity highlighting aromas and flavors of mineral-rich citrus and citrus peel, mango and kiwi fruits. Generous, mouth-filling and long. Drink now–2012. Score 90.

HAGAFEN, SAUVIGNON BLANC, NAPA VALLEY, 2006: Light golden straw in color, certainly one of the best dry whites to date from Hagafen. As many of the Hagafen wines, opens with a complex and concentrated nose, in this case showing citrus and grapes, those going in a few moments to orange peel and hints of mango and freshly mown grass. On the palate a tempting array of mixed citrus and citrus peel, those with an underlying hint of bitterness that is set off nicely by lively acidity. Drink now. Score 91.

HAGAFEN, ROUSSANNE, RIPKEN VINEYARD, NAPA VALLEY, 2007:
Blended with 15% of Marsanne grapes, a white somewhere in personality between California and the Rhone. Deeply aromatic, medium-bodied and showing an appealing array of citrus and tropical fruits, those supported nicely by hints of green tea, bitter orange peel and spring flowers. Drink now–2013. Score 90.

HAGAFEN, WHITE RIESLING, 30TH ANNIVERSARY, DEVOTO VINEYARDS, LAKE COUNTY, 2008: Golden straw in color, with moderate sweetness set off nicely by balancing acidity, opens to reveal ripe apricot, white peach and pineapple fruits, those supported by a tantalizing hint of mint. Long and generous, best as an aperitif. Drink now–2013. Score 90.

HAGAFEN, WHITE RIESLING, 30TH ANNIVERSARY, MAYERI VINEYARD, NAPA VALLEY, 2008: Light golden straw in color, medium-bodied, with generous sweetness and deeply aromatic, opening to reveal a generous array of aromas and flavors, those including ripe white peaches, apricots, grapefruit and papaya. Rich and generous. Give this one some time and it will develop an appealing petrol note. Approachable and enjoyable now but best 2011–2016. Score 91.

HAGAFEN, WHITE RIESLING, MAYERI VINEYARD, NAPA VALLEY, 2007: A crisply dry Riesling, showing a vague and tantalizing hint of sweetness. Light straw in color, on the nose showing generous tropical and summer fruits, those matched on the palate with notes of cherries and red berries. Medium-bodied with a long, near bitter-sweet finish. In a word, lovely. Drink now–2011. Score 90.

Don Ernesto Series

HAGAFEN, CRESCENDO, RED TABLE WINE, DON ERNESTO, NAPA VALLEY, 2003: A garnet-red blend of Cabernet Sauvignon and Cabernet Franc, medium- to full-bodied, with soft tannins now integrated nicely and showing a spicy cherry-berry and currant personality. Drink now. Score 87.

HAGAFEN, COLLAGE, WHITE TABLE WINE, DON ERNESTO, COLLAGE, NORTH COAST, 2006: Light golden straw in color, a blend of 85% Marsanne and 15% Roussanne grapes, opens with a light musky aroma that calls to mind the Rhone, that blowing off quickly to reveal a potpourri of lemon, lime, papaya and mango aromas and flavors. Nothing complex here but lingers nicely on the finish and an excellent summertime quaffer. Drink up. Score 87.

Herzog Wine Cellars ✶✶✶✶✶

Herzog: Generation VIII, Special Edition and Special Reserve Series

HERZOG, CABERNET SAUVIGNON, GENERATION VIII, TO KALON, NAPA VALLEY, 2006: A single-vineyard release, at this stage of its development a literal blockbuster, almost impenetrably dark garnet in color, opening with firm tannins and nearly intense spices and oak. Given time in the glass shows fine balance and structure, the wood and tannins yielding to blackcurrants, blackberries, and an abundance of chocolate, all lingering long and comfortably on the palate. Give this one the time it deserves and it will show black cherry and perhaps even notes of raspberries and red licorice, the winemaker wisely letting the terroir of the vineyard show its best. Destined for polished elegance. Drink now if you must, but best from 2011–2018, perhaps longer. Score 94.

HERZOG, CABERNET SAUVIGNON, GENERATION VIII, NORTH COAST, CALIFORNIA, 2004: Made entirely from Cabernet Sauvignon grapes from Napa and the Chalk Hill's Warnecke vineyard, oak aged for 23 months in French oak. Showing spicy and toasty oak notes and softly mouth-coating tannins, and opening to reveal a fine array of blackberry, currant and red plum aromas and flavors, those supported nicely by hints of espresso coffee and vanilla. Long and generous. Drink now–2012. Score 91.

HERZOG, CABERNET SAUVIGNON, SINGLE VINEYARD, HAYSTACK PEAK VINEYARD, ATLAS PEAK, 2007: Dark, intense and concentrated, but maintaining its stylishness and elegance. Oak aged for 14 months, showing medium- to full-bodied (leaning towards the full), with hints of grilled herbs and black olives that play nicely together with ripe currant and black cherry fruits. As the wine matures look for notes of tobacco and graphite here, those settling in to a very long and satisfying finish. Best from release–2015, perhaps longer. Score 93.

HERZOG, CABERNET SAUVIGNON, SPECIAL RESERVE, ALEXANDER VALLEY, 2005: Deeply aromatic, full-bodied, with silky tannins settling in nicely to show a gentle hand with the wood. On the nose and palate blackberries, blackcurrants and purple plums, those matched nicely by notes of spicy cedarwood. Long and elegant. Drink now–2013. Score 91.

HERZOG, CABERNET SAUVIGNON, SPECIAL RESERVE, NAPA VALLEY, 2005: Dark garnet, medium- to full-bodied, with soft tannins and lightly spicy wood integrated nicely to highlight traditional Cabernet aromas and flavors of blackcurrant, blackberry and black cherry fruits, those complemented nicely by notes of toasted rye bread and, on the long finish, notes of Oriental spices. Drink now–2011. Score 90.

HERZOG, CABERNET SAUVIGNON, SPECIAL EDITION, WARNECKE VINEYARD, CHALK HILL, SONOMA, 2005: Deep, almost inky garnet in color, full-bodied, showing generous but gently mouth-coating tannins. With a nose redolent of dark chocolate, licorice and berries, opens to reveal a generous array of currant and blackberry fruits, those highlighted by notes of black pepper and Oriental spices and, on the long finish, an appealing hint of eucalyptus. Rich and concentrated. Drink now–2013. Score 92.

HERZOG, CABERNET SAUVIGNON, SPECIAL RESERVE, NAPA VALLEY, 2004: Deep garnet in color, full-bodied, with still firm tannins needing a bit of time to settle down but those already showing fine balance with spicy wood and opening to rich and elegant aromas and flavors of currants and berry fruits, those supported nicely by hints of juniper berries and black pepper. On the long finish a tantalizing hint of what at one moment seems to be dark chocolate and at the next licorice. Drink now–2012. Score 92.

HERZOG, CABERNET SAUVIGNON, SPECIAL RESERVE, ALEXANDER VALLEY, 2004: Medium- to full-bodied, with near-sweet cedarwood and chocolate on the nose, opening to reveal firm tannins, those now integrating nicely. Look for aromas and flavors of currants, black cherries and Mediterranean herbs, those leading to a moderately-long finish on which you will find a nice hint of dark cocoa. Drink now–2011. Score 90.

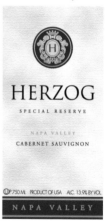

HERZOG, CABERNET SAUVIGNON, SPECIAL EDITION, CHALK HILL, WARNECKE VINEYARD, SONOMA, 2004: Full-bodied, with soft, gently mouth-coating tannins and appealing spices and vanilla from the barriques in which it aged. Shows a generous array of blackcurrant, blackberry and blueberry fruits, those on a tempting background of cigar tobacco and chocolate. Drink now. Score 91.

HERZOG, CABERNET SAUVIGNON, SPECIAL RESERVE, NAPA VALLEY, 2003: Dark ruby towards royal purple, supple and elegant, showing soft, well-integrated tannins, and a gentle hand with the oak revealing sweet cedarwood. Opening nicely in the glass to reveal blackberry, black cherry and currant fruits. Elegant and long, with a fruity and softly tannic finish. Drink now–2011. Score 91.

HERZOG, CABERNET SAUVIGNON, SPECIAL RESERVE, ALEXANDER VALLEY, 2003: Dark garnet in color, tight and compact on first attack but opening in the glass to reveal its full-body, firm tannins and generous spicy oak, those yielding slowly to black fruits (currants, berries and cherries) on a background of Mediterranean herbs. On the long finish, appealing hints of chocolate and mint. Drink now–2011. Score 89.

HERZOG, CABERNET SAUVIGNON, GENERATION VIII, NORTH COAST, 2002: Dark garnet with orange and purple reflections, full-bodied, with once firm tannins now integrated nicely. Needing a bit more time to settle down but already showing fine balance and structure. Reflecting its 23 months in French oak with spices and toasty wood, those opening to reveal generous plum, red berry and espresso coffee notes. On the lingering and mouth-filling finish, nice hints of white chocolate. Drink now–2012. Score 92.

HERZOG, CABERNET SAUVIGNON, SPECIAL EDITION, CHALK HILL WARNECKE VINEYARD, 2002: Lots of oak here but that well balanced by soft tannins and appealing layers of fruit and herbs. On the nose and palate look for cassis, berry and black cherry fruits, those backed up nicely by vanilla and hints of anise and bitter orange peel that play nicely on the palate. Long, round and satisfying. Drink now. Score 90.

HERZOG, MERLOT, SPECIAL RESERVE, AL-EXANDER VALLEY, 2006: Full-bodied, with generous oak influences and soft tannins in fine proportion to fruits and acidity. On first attack black fruits, those yielding comfortably to notes of wild berries and espresso coffee and, on the finish, hints of strawberries and milk chocolate. Long and mouth-filling. Drink now–2011. Score 90.

HERZOG, MERLOT, SPECIAL RESERVE, ALEXANDER VALLEY, 2005: Garnet towards royal purple, medium-bodied, with soft tannins and a gentle hint of spicy oak. On the nose and palate blackberries, blueberries and cassis, those complemented by hints of spices, vanilla and white pepper. Drink now. Score 89.

HERZOG, MERLOT, SPECIAL RESERVE, ALEXANDER VALLEY, 2003: Deep ruby towards royal purple in color, medium- to full-bodied, with soft, mouth-coating, near-sweet tannins and hints of spicy and vanilla-rich oak. Opens on the palate showing aromas and flavors of blueberries and blackberries on a light peppery background. Drink now. Score 89.

HERZOG, SYRAH, SPECIAL RESERVE, EDNA VALLEY, 2005: Full-bodied, with generous wood and tannins integrated nicely to highlight and not hide aromas and flavors of red berries, cherries, peppermint and spring flowers, those complemented by notes of peppermint and spicy oak. A long and generous finish. Drink now–2012. Score 90.

HERZOG, SYRAH, SPECIAL RESERVE, EDNA VALLEY, SOUTH COAST, 2003: Dark garnet towards royal purple, full-bodied and with somewhat chunky tannins only now starting to settle down. Moderate vanilla, spices and meatiness from the wood and the grapes to highlight blackberry, blueberry and espresso coffee aromas and flavors. Drink now–2012. Score 89.

HERZOG, PINOT NOIR, SPECIAL RESERVE, EDNA VALLEY, 2006: Garnet towards royal purple, medium-bodied, with soft tannins and a gentle hint of wood. On the nose and palate wild berry, black and red cherries, and a hint of lightly toasted rye bread. Drink now–2012. Score 89.

HERZOG, PINOT NOIR, SPECIAL RESERVE, EDNA VALLEY, 2005: Ruby towards garnet, medium-bodied, a delicate Burgundy-style wine showing gently caressing tannins and opening to reveal cherry, wild berry and light spices, all lingering long and comfortably. Drink now–2012. Score 90.

HERZOG, PINOT NOIR, SPECIAL RESERVE, EDNA VALLEY, SOUTH COAST, CALIFORNIA, 2005: Medium-bodied, with good extraction and soft but mouth-coating tannins, reflecting eight months' development partly in barriques with nice hints of toasted white bread. On the nose and palate raspberries and wild berries with appealing herbal and light earthy overtones. Drink now. Score 89.

HERZOG, ZINFANDEL, SPECIAL RESERVE, LODI, 2006: Dark garnet, full-bodied, deep and concentrated, with still intense tannins and wood waiting to settle down but showing fine balance and structure that bode well for the future. On the nose and palate blackberry, purple plum, spices and peppermint, all coming together in a long, mouth-filling finish. Drink now–2012. Score 90.

HERZOG, ZINFANDEL, SPECIAL RESERVE, LODI, 2005: Deep royal purple in color, medium- to full-bodied, with soft tannins integrated nicely and showing appealing spicy plum and berry fruits. Long and generous. Drink now. Score 88.

HERZOG, PETITE SIRAH, LIMITED EDITION, LODI, 2005: Opens with a near-sweet plum and berry nose, goes on to reveal full body with somewhat rustic, country-style tannins. On the nose and palate intense and peppery with generous wild berry, dried date and cedary wood notes, those supported by a hint of vanilla that runs through to the long finish. Drink now–2011. Score 89.

HERZOG, CABERNET SAUVIGNON, ZINFANDEL-SYRAH, SPECIAL RESERVE, CALIFORNIA, 2005: As has become the tradition, a wine based on grapes from three different vineyards (Napa, Watts and Edna Valley this year). A blend of 66% Cabernet Sauvignon, 31% Zinfandel and 3% Syrah, each grape vinified separately in American oak for about 14 months and then blended before bottling. Full-bodied, with still firm tannins needing time in the glass to settle down, and generous vanilla and toast from the wood, opening to show generous wild berries, blackcurrants and purple plums, those on an appealingly spicy background. Drink now–2012. Score 90.

HERZOG, CHARDONNAY, SPECIAL RESERVE, RUSSIAN RIVER VALLEY, 2006: Light gold with orange tints, full-bodied, with generous oak and citrus on first attack, those opening to reveal appealing nutty and stony mineral overlays, all leading to a near-buttery finish. Drink now. Score 89.

Herzog: Late Harvest Wines

HERZOG, CHENIN BLANC, LATE HARVEST, CLARKSBURG, 2007: Light gold with orange tints, full-bodied and generously sweet with good acidity to keep the wine lively. A fine effort, rich and generous, with dried apricot and yellow peaches on first attack, those yielding to notes of mango and ginger, all overlaid with light hints of ginger and blanched almonds. Long and generous. Fine with goose liver dishes or as a dessert wine. Drink now–2013, perhaps longer. Score 90.

HERZOG, WHITE RIESLING, LATE HARVEST, MONTEREY COUNTY, 2007: Moderate sweetness set off by good balancing acidity and showing rich floral, citrus and citrus peel and caramel notes, those supported nicely by spicy and light petrol notes. Concentrated and well done. Drink now–2014. Score 91.

Herzog: Baron Herzog Series

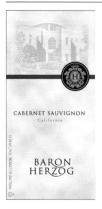

BARON HERZOG, CABERNET SAUVIGNON, CENTRAL COAST, 2006: Lightly oaked, dark garnet in color, full-bodied and with caressing tannins. On the nose and palate appealing wild berry, blackcurrant and licorice notes, all lingering nicely on the finish. Drink now–2011. Score 88.

BARON HERZOG, MERLOT, PASO ROBLES, 2005: Medium- to full-bodied, garnet towards royal purple in color, with soft, well-integrated oak and gently mouth-coating tannins. On the nose and palate red currants, wild berries, and notes of espresso coffee. Long and generous. Drink now. Score 88.

BARON HERZOG, SYRAH/SHIRAZ, CALIFORNIA, 2007: So named, I suppose, to avoid or add to the confusion on the part of Americans, but that's fair enough. Dark royal purple, medium-bodied, with soft tannins and a gentle hand with the oak and showing an array of blackberries, blueberries and currants, those with notes of spicy oak and, on the moderately long finish, a hint of bittersweet chocolate. Drink now–2011. Score 88.

BARON HERZOG, CHENIN BLANC, CLARKSVILLE, 2007: Ripe and forward, with melon, apple, peach and gooseberry fruits. Light golden in color, medium-bodied and with a fruit-forward nose leading to a round, lightly nutty finish. Drink now. Score 88.

Herzog: Weinstock Series

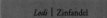

WEINSTOCK, ZINFANDEL, CELLAR SE-LECT, LODI, 2004: Blended with a small amount of Cabernet Sauvignon, starts off rather harshly on the palate, but don't let that discourage you, for after a few minutes in the glass the tannins soften and the initial almost searing intensity recedes nicely. The deep tannins part to reveal generous jammy berries and leathery, almost gamey notes along with hints of pepper, tobacco and bittersweet chocolate. Drinking beautifully now but not for much further cellaring. Drink now. Score 89.

WEINSTOCK, CELLAR SELECTION, SAUVIGNON BLANC, CENTRAL COAST, 2007: Dark golden straw in color, with fresh aromas and flavors of citrus, apricots and apples on first attack, those going to pear and red grapefruit and hints of spice and eucalyptus. Drink now. Score 88.

New York State

Red Fern Cellars ***

RED FERN CELLARS, CABERNET SAUVIGNON, LONG ISLAND, N.Y., 2005: Dark garnet towards royal purple, medium- to full-bodied, with gently mouth-coating tannins, opening to reveal a blackberry-blackcurrant profile, the fruits matched by notes of black pepper, anise and, on the moderately-long finish, a note of demerara sugar. Drink now–2012. Score 88.

RED FERN CELLARS, MERLOT, LONG ISLAND, N.Y., 2005: Light garnet in color, light- to medium-bodied, with softly caressing tannins and aromas and flavors of cherries, blackberries and blueberries, those highlighted by hints of anise and freshly ground coffee. Not overly complex but a good match to food. Drink now–2011. Score 88.

RED FERN CELLARS, MERLOT, LONG ISLAND, N.Y., 2004: Dark ruby towards garnet, full-bodied, with once gripping tannins now settling in nicely. On the nose and palate near jammy black cherries and blackberries, those rich with spices and earthy mineral overtones and, on the long spicy finish, a hint of strong tea. Drink now–2010. Score 88.

RED FERN CELLARS, SYRAH, LONG ISLAND, N.Y., 2005: Dark garnet in color, medium- to full-bodied, with gripping tannins that need some time to settle down. Opens slowly in the glass to reveal blackberries, black cherries and bittersweet chocolate, those followed by notes of wildflowers and sage. Drink now–2012. Score 89.

RED FERN CELLARS, CHARDONNAY, LONG ISLAND, N.Y., 2005: Glistening gold in color, medium- to full-bodied, with generous oak but that set off nicely by lively acidity. On the nose and palate generous citrus, citrus peel and citrus flowers, those with an appealing creamy texture that fills the mouth nicely. On the finish, a welcome note of stony minerals. Drink now–2011. Score 89.

ITALY

BARTENURA, CHIANTI, 2006: Ruby towards garnet, medium-bodied, with soft tannins, a simple but pleasant wine, round and easy to drink, showing berries, cherries and a light peppery overtone. Not complex but a good quaffer. Drink now. Score 85.

MONTE OLIVO, OPINIONI, UMBRIA ROSSO, 2005: A medium- to full-bodied blend of equal parts of Merlot and Cabernet Sauvignon. Soft, near-sweet tannins highlight lightly spicy aromas and flavors of currants and blackberries, those matched by a hint of cured cigar tobacco and dark chocolate. Round and appealing. Drink now. Score 86.

RASHI, BARBERA D'ALBA, PIEDMONT, 2006: Ruby towards garnet, medium-bodied, with gently caressing tannins and opening to show appealing red and black berries, those on a background of minted dark chocolate. A lovely Barbera. Drink now. Score 88.

RASHI, PINOT GRIGIO, VENETO, 2005: Light golden straw in color, with crisp acidity and showing aromas and flavors of lemon rind, green apples and flinty minerals. Fresh and refreshing but not for further cellaring. Drink up. Score 86.

RASHI, MALVASIA, PUGLIA, 2005: A semi-dry red, but one with good balancing acidity to keep it lively and showing generous strawberry, cranberry and raspberry notes. Light and easy to drink. Drink up. Score 85.

RASHI, MOSCATO D'ASTI, 2007: Light, semi-sweet and lightly *frizzante*, showing appealing pear, green apple and citrus notes. Not complex but lively and refreshing. Drink up. Score 85.

RASHI, BARBERA D'ASTI, PIEDMONT, 2006: Dark ruby red, light- to medium-bodied, with appealing notes of wild berries, cassis and citrus peel. A good quaffing wine, especially if served lightly chilled. Drink up. Score 85.

S'FORNO, PINOT GRIGIO, VENETO, 2006: Light straw colored, light- to medium-bodied, with lively acidity to show appealing grapefruit, melon and mineral notes. Crisply dry, a good entry-level white. Drink up. Score 85.

PORTUGAL

CASA DA CORCA, DOURO, PORTUGAL, 2005: Garnet towards royal purple, medium-bodied, reflecting its ten months in barriques with gently spicy wood and soft, well-integrated tannins. An oak-aged blend of Touriga Nacional, Tinta Roriz and Touriga Franca, showing blackberry, currant and licorice notes, those yielding on the finish to hints

of espresso coffee. Generous and mouth-filling. Drink now. Score 88.

CASA DA CORCA, RESERVA, DOURO, PORTUGAL, 2004: Dark ruby towards garnet, medium-bodied, with somewhat chunky country-style tannins. Opens to show smoky oak, plum, wild berry and currant fruits, those on a background that hints of eucalyptus and green olives. Drink now. Score 86.

SPAIN

CAPCANES, FLOR DI PRIMAVERA/PERAJ HA'ABIB, MONSANT, CATALUNYA, SPAIN, 2006: A traditional blend of Garnacha, Cabernet Sauvignon and Carinena (Carignan). Full-bodied, with firm tannins and generous spicy wood, those integrating nicely and showing fine balance and structure that bode well for the future. Showing a generous array of blackcurrants, wild berries and purple plums on a background that hints at one moment of Oriental spices, at the next of freshly roasted coffee, and at yet the next of dark chocolate. Intriguing, complex and long. Approachable now, but best 2011–2016. Score 91.

CAPCANES, FLOR DI PRIMAVERA/PERAJ HA'ABIB, MONSANT, CATALUNYA, SPAIN, 2005: A full-bodied, dark garnet towards royal purple blend of Garnacha, Cabernet Sauvignon and Carinena, showing firm tannins, those already integrating nicely with spicy wood and black fruits. On first attack blackcurrants and purple plums, those followed by blueberries, spices and Mediterranean herbs. Remains one of the best kosher wines of Europe. Drink now–2016. Score 92.

CAPCANES, FLOR DI PRIMAVERA/PERAJ HA'ABIB, MONSANT, CATALUNYA, SPAIN, 2004: A blend this year of 35% each Garnacha and Cabernet Sauvignon with 30% of Carinena. Super-dark garnet reflecting in part a 42-day maceration period, with still firm tannins needing time to settle down but with balance and structure that bode well for the future. Opens with spicy wood that quickly subsides to show plum and currant fruits, those complemented well by white pepper, sweet herbs and a light mineral note on the finish. Drink now–2015. Score 92.

CAPCANES, FLOR DE PRIMAVERA/PERAJ HA'ABIB, MONSANT, CATALUNYA, SPAIN 2003: A blend of Garnacha, Cabernet Sauvignon, Carinena and Tempranillo (40%, 35%, 20% and 5% respectively) aged in new and one-year-old French barriques for about 12 months. Now showing dark ruby towards garnet, with once firm tannins integrating nicely with wood, acidity and fruits. On the nose and palate blackcurrant, cherry and raspberry fruits matched well by overlays of coffee, licorice and a generous hint of minerals. On the long finish look as well for a hint of peppermint. Drink now–2012. Score 92.

CAPCANES, PERAJ PETITA, MONSANT, CATALUNYA, SPAIN, 2007: Dark garnet, medium- to full-bodied, with silky tannins integrating nicely and showing an appealing hint of spicy wood. A blend of Garnacha, Tempranillo and Samso, opens to reveal appealing red and black berries and cassis fruits, those supported nicely by notes of minerals and chocolate. Drink now–2012. Score 90.

CAPCANES, PERAJ PETITA, MONSANT, CATALUNYA, SPAIN, 2006: Think of this as the second wine of Capcanes if you will, but whereas that wine goes for depth, concentration and aging potential, this lighter wine is destined for earlier and easier drinking. Developed primarily in stainless steel, with only 15% oak-aged, this medium-bodied, ruby towards garnet blend of Garnacha del Pais, Tempranillo (known in the region as Ull de Llebre) and Samso (the local name for Carinena or Carignan), shows soft tannins integrating nicely and with generous raspberry, red plum, cassis and cola aromas and flavors, those with an appealing mineral overlay and just the barest hint of sweetness on the long finish. Drink now–2011. Score 90.

BODEGAS CASA QUEMADA, TEMPRANILLO, TIERRA DE CASTILLA, 2007: Dark cherry red towards garnet in color, medium-bodied, with soft, almost plush tannins. Reflecting its six months in oak with vanilla and light smoky notes, opening to show a nose and palate of sweet cherries, berries and sweet cedar notes. Generous and fresh, with notes of dark chocolate rising on the finish. Drink now–2012. Score 88.

ELVI, CLASSICO, RIBERA DEL JUCAR, 2007: A garnet red, medium-bodied blend of 87% Tempranillo and 13% Merlot showing lightly gripping tannins and a hint of spicy wood. On the nose and palate plum, blackberry, earthy and smoky aromas and **Elvi, Ness, Ribera del Jucar, 2007:** Garnet red, medium- to full-bodied and unoaked, with soft tannins, a blend of Cabernet Sauvignon, Tempranillo and Syrah. On the nose and palate blackberry, currant and purple plum fruits on a lightly spicy background hinting of vanilla and sweet cedarwood. Drink now. Score 86.

ELVI, MATIZ, RIOJA, 2007: Made entirely from Tempranillo grapes, an aromatic and expressive wine. Medium-bodied, with soft tannins integrating nicely and showing generous black cherry, kirsch and spicy notes. Lingers nicely. Drink now–2011. Score 87.

ELVI, VINA ENCINA, RIBERA DEL JUCAR, 2007: A gently oaked blend of Bobal, Merlot and Cabernet Sauvignon grapes. Medium-bodied, with soft tannins and an appealing array of black cherry, currant and blackberry fruits, those supported nicely by hints of chocolate and cigar tobacco. Drink now–2012. Score 88.

ELVI, VINA ENCINA, RIBERA DEL JUCAR, 2004: Medium-dark ruby towards garnet, medium-bodied and gently oaked, a blend of equal parts of Tempranillo, Bobal and Cabernet Sauvignon. On the nose and palate red plums, blackberries, hints of smoky oak and a lightly earthy overtone. Drink now. Score 86.

ELVI, MAKOR, UTIEL-REQUIA, 2006: Made entirely from Bobal grapes, a medium-bodied red with chunky, country-style tannins that smooths out on the palate to show a basic cherry-berry personality, the fruits on a near-sweet cedar and tobacco background. Drink now. Score 85.

ELVI 26, PRIORAT, 2005: A blend of Syrah, Grenache, Cabernet Sauvignon and Merlot. Full-bodied, with mouth-coating tannins and a generous dose of spicy oak, those in fine balance with jammy blackberry, purple plum and cassis notes. Muscular but with elegance. Drink now–2014. Score 88.

RAMON CORDOVA, RESERVA, RIOJA, 2001: Made, as are most of the Cordova wines, entirely from Tempranillo grapes. Medium- to full-bodied, dark garnet in color, its once firm tannins now settled in comfortably, showing appealing blackberry, purple plum and currant fruits. Drink now. Score 86.

TERRENAL, CABERNET SAUVIGNON, YECLA, SPAIN, 2005: A pleasant little country-style wine, medium-bodied, with somewhat chunky tannins and showing appealing berry and black cherry fruits. Not complex but a good quaffer. Drink now. Score 85.

TERRENAL, MERLOT, YECLA, SPAIN, 2006: Soft and round, an internationalized little Merlot but a pleasant enough one, showing medium-bodied, with soft tannins and a berry-black cherry personality. Drink now. Score 85.

AUSTRALIA AND NEW ZEALAND

Australia

BECKETT'S FLAT, CABERNET SAUVIGNON-SHIRAZ, MARGARET RIVER, WESTERN AUSTRALIA, 2003: Dense and chewy when first poured but opening beautifully in the glass to reveal a wine that becomes soft and round, with a broad array of black cherry, currant, tar and peppery flavors and aromas. Drink up. Score 88.

BECKETT'S FLAT, SHIRAZ, FIVE STONES, WESTERN AUSTRALIA, 2006: Dark garnet, medium- to full-bodied, with gripping tannins that open in the glass to show currant, plum and black cherry fruits, those with an appealing peppery overlay. Drink now. Score 87.

BECKETT'S FLAT, SHIRAZ, MARGARET RIVER, WESTERN AUSTRALIA, 2003: Medium- to full-bodied, smooth and rich, with primary aromas and flavors of plums, blackberries and spices, those with light overlays of cola. Soft tannins, just the mildest hint of sweet cedar and an overall fine balance let the flavors make themselves felt and linger nicely. Drink up. Score 88.

TEAL LAKE, SHIRAZ, RESERVE, S.E. AUSTRALIA, 2004: In its youth soft, round and not complex but quite pleasant, showing medium-bodied, with soft tannins and appealing cherry, berry and spicy aromas. Now sliding past its peak and starting to show age. Drink up. Score 86.

TEAL LAKE, CABERNET-MERLOT, S.E. AUSTRALIA, 2007: Dark garnet, medium- to full-bodied with gently mouth-coating tannins and a light note of sweet cedarwood. Opens to reveal flavors and aromas of currants, plums, licorice and anise, all leading to a moderately long finish. Drink now. Score 87.

TEAL LAKE, SHIRAZ, S.E. AUSTRALIA, 2007: Dark garnet, medium- to full-bodied with chunky, country-style tannins but opening in the glass to show generous cherry, berry and plum fruits, those on a lightly spicy background, the flavors lingering nicely. Drink now. Score 86.

TEAL LAKE, CHARDONNAY, S.E. AUSTRALIA, 2008: Light golden straw in color, medium-bodied, with crisp acidity to highlight citrus and tropical fruits. Nothing complex here but a very pleasant quaffer. Drink now. Score 86.

New Zealand

GOOSE BAY, PINOT NOIR, EAST COAST, NEW ZEALAND, 2007: Light ruby towards cherry in color, light towards medium-bodied, an easy to drink little red with soft tannins and berry, cherry and cassis notes. Light enough on the palate that you might think it was a rosé. Not complex but a good entry level quaffer. Drink now. Score 86.

GOOSE BAY, PINOT NOIR, EAST COAST, NEW ZEALAND, 2006: Cherry red towards garnet, medium-bodied, with super-soft tannins and showing cherry, raspberry and strawberry fruits on a lightly spicy and cedary-oak background. A not overly complex wine, but a very pleasant quaffer. Drink now. Score 86.

GOOSE BAY, PINOT NOIR, MARL-BOROUGH, NEW ZEALAND, 2006: Dark ruby in color, medium-bodied, with soft tannins and just a hint of spicy wood. Opens to show appealing raspberry, cassis and orange peel, those supported nicely by hints of white pepper. As pleasant with fish and seafood as with chicken and light veal dishes. Drink now. Score 87.

GOOSE BAY, CHARDONNAY, MARLBOROUGH, NEW ZEALAND, 2006: Deep golden in color, medium- to full-bodied, with a generous overlay of vanilla crème patisserie that parts to reveal apricot, peach and citrus-like acidity and minerality that keep the wine lively. A generous floral and fruity finish. Drink now. Score 87.

GOOSE BAY, SAUVIGNON BLANC, MARLBOROUGH, NEW ZEALAND, 2007: Light straw in color, with distinct gooseberry, green apple and tropical fruits all on a background of freshly mown grass. Medium-bodied, round, with good balancing acidity, an appealing quaffer. Drink now. Score 86.

GOOSE BAY, VIOGNIER, MARLBOROUGH, NEW ZEALAND, 2007: Bright and lively, medium-bodied, with fine balancing acidity to highlight aromas and flavors of white peaches, apples and spring flowers. Just enough complexity here to grab our attention. Drink now. Score 87.

GOOSE BAY, PINOT GRIS, EAST COAST, NEW ZEALAND, 2007: Fresh and appealing, medium-bodied, with nectarine, pear and melon fruits along with a hint of citrus peel. Drink now. Score 87.

SOUTH AFRICA

BACKSBERG, MERLOT, PAARL, COASTAL, SOUTH AFRICA, 2007: Garnet towards royal purple, medium- to full-bodied, with soft, near-sweet tannins in fine balance with notes of fruit and spicy wood. On first attack a distinct raspberry flavor, that followed by plums and cherries, all supported nicely by notes of freshly roasted herbs. Drink now–2011. Score 88.

BACKSBERG, PINOTAGE, PAARL, COASTAL, SOUTH AFRICA, 2007: Ruby towards garnet, medium-bodied, with soft tannins and a light note of vanilla from the oak in which the wine was partly developed. On the nose and palate cherry, blackcurrant, purple plum and hints of raisins. Not overly complex but easy to drink. Drink now. Score 86.

SOUTH AMERICA

Argentina

BODEGAS FLECHAS DE LOS ANDES, GRAN MALBEC, MENDOZA, ARGENTINA, 2008: A joint project by Benjamin de Rothschild and Laurent Dessault of Château Dessault. Dark garnet towards youthful royal purple, full-bodied, with generous but soft tannins and spicy wood settling down and showing good balance and structure. Opens to reveal appealing blueberries and figs, those supported nicely by hints of dark minted chocolate. Long and satisfying. Drink now–2011. Score 89.

BODEGAS FLECHAS DE LOS ANDES, GRAN MALBEC, MENDOZA, ARGENTINA, 2007: Garnet towards youthful royal purple, medium-bodied, with soft, gently mouth-coating tannins and opening to reveal purple plum, black cherry and red currant fruits, those on a lightly spicy background, and finishing with a hint of licorice. A very good match to spicy sausages and grilled beef or lamb. Drink now–2011. Score 87.

TERRENAL, CABERNET SAUVIGNON, MENDOZA, ARGENTINA, 2006: Dark ruby towards garnet, with soft tannins, hints of spices and a note of chocolate highlighting blackberry and black cherry fruits. Round and appealing, a very good entry-level wine. Drink now. Score 86.

TIERRA SALVAJE, MERLOT, MENDOZA, ARGENTINA, 2007: Dark garnet, medium-bodied, with near-sweet tannins and just a hint of spicy wood. Opens in the glass to show plum, blackberry and citrus peel notes. A fine entry level quaffer. Drink now. Score 85.

Chile

ALFASI, MERLOT, MAULE VALLEY, CHILE, 2007: A somewhat internationalized Merlot, but pleasant enough, with medium body, a light oak influence and soft tannins to support black cherry and plum notes. Smooth and round, a good quaffer. Drink now. Score 85.

ALFASI, MALBEC-SYRAH RESERVE, MAULE VALLEY, CHILE, 2007:

A blend of equal parts of Malbec and Syrah grapes, medium- to full-bodied, with gently mouth-coating tannins and a light touch of vanilla-rich wood. On the nose and palate black cherry, damson plums and a light note of candied orange peel come together nicely, those backed up by notes of white chocolate and espresso coffee. Long and rich, with a hint of dried raisins on the finish. Drink now. Score 89.

ALFASI, CHARDONNAY, MAULE VALLEY, CHILE, 2007: Light golden straw in color, medium-bodied, with crisp minerality and acidity to highlight pineapple, citrus and mango fruits. Not complex but very pleasant and easy to drink. Drink up. Score 86.

ALFASI, SAUVIGNON BLANC, LATE HARVEST, MAULE VALLEY, CHILE, 2001: A bit confusing because the label identifies this as made from Sauvignon Blanc grapes and information received from the producer indicates that it is a blend of Sauvignon Blanc and Semillon. Whatever the case, this is a medium- to full-bodied dessert wine, now going to bronzed gold, with just the right notes of botrytis funkiness. On the nose and palate dried apricots and honeyed apple notes. Good balance here between moderate sweetness and acidity and, on the generous finish, an appealing note of caramel. Drink now. Score 88.

DON ALFONSO, CABERNET SAUVIGNON, MAULE VALLEY, CHILE, 2006: Dark garnet, medium- to full-bodied, with spicy oak and somewhat chunky country-style tannins, opens in the glass to reveal a basic berry-cherry personality, that with hints of earthy minerals and cigar tobacco. Drink now. Score 85.

TERROSO, CHARDONNAY, LONTUE VALLEY, CHILE, 2008: Light gold in color with orange reflections, medium-bodied with generous apple and fig fruits and a near creamy finish, all with an appealing light yeasty overlay. Drink now. Score 87.

TERROSO, CHARDONNAY, MAULE VALLEY, CHILE, 2007: Gold, taking on a light bronzed note, a medium-bodied and lively white with lightly spicy citrus, pear and green apples, the fruits taking on a bit of a fruit-compote nature. Still drinking well but not for further cellaring. Drink up. Score 86.

TIERRA SALVAJE, CABERNET SAUVIGNON, LONTUE VALLEY, CHILE, 2008: Garnet towards royal purple, medium-bodied, with soft tannins, opening to show blackberry and black cherry fruits, those complemented by hints of tobacco and roasted coffee. Drink now. Score 86.

TIERRA SALVAJE, CHARDONNAY, MAULE VALLEY, CHILE, 2007: Straightforward but very pleasing, with appealing pear, apple and citrus flavors and a generous mineral hint. Not overly complex but quite pleasant. Drink now. Score 86.

TIERRA SALVAJE, SAUVIGNON BLANC, LONTUE VALLEY, CHILE, 2008: Light straw colored, light- to medium-bodied, with an appealing array of lemon, lime, red grapefruit and chive flavors. Crisply dry, with fine balance between fruits and acidity giving the wine a "zingy" finish. Drink now. Score 87.

TIERRA SALVAJE, SAUVIGNON BLANC, MAULE VALLEY, CHILE, 2007: The color of damp straw, medium-bodied, with lime and grapefruit notes supported by hints of sweet peas and freshly cut grass. Drink up. Score 86.

THE WINES AND THE WINERIES: ROSÉ, DESSERT AND SPARKLING WINES

Champagne and Sparkling Wines

For many hundreds of years, the wine most often associated with the superior way of life has been Champagne. Attributed a soul, temperament and wit, many Frenchmen are convinced that Champagne can do them no harm, no matter how much they consume. Madame de Pompadour declared that "it is the only wine that makes a woman more beautiful after drinking." This delightful beverage is so much a cultural phenomenon in France that a person who dislikes Champagne is pitied, or regarded as sick, disabled or depraved.

In 1688, when the Benedictine monk Dom Perignon was placed in charge of the wine cellars of the Abbey of Hautvilliers near Epernay, his odd ideas about making wine had his colleagues wondering whether he was a clairvoyant, a saint or something of a madman. If one accepts the popular mythology, this untutored chemist had the brilliant idea of adding small amounts of yeast and sugar to bottles of wine. This led to a secondary fermentation which in turn released gas under pressure into the wine. Dom Perignon had discovered a way to make wine sparkle, and since then sparkling Champagne has become the source for an entire mythology. It goes without saying that only wines that come from the Champagne region of France are entitled to be called "Champagne." All other wines, even those made by what has come to be known as the *methode champenoise,* are properly referred to as "sparkling wines."

Making Champagne is a lengthy process. Fermented grape juices, the produce of many different vineyards, are blended and then bottled with a mixture of sugar and yeast to induce a second fermentation. This produces carbon dioxide which, since it is sealed in, dissolves in the wine and creates the fizz. Since the yeast forms an ugly deposit, the bottles are stored with their heads down and are turned occasionally, thereby forcing this deposit to flow downwards towards the corks. This process is known as *riddling*. Towards the end of the process, which takes anywhere from six months to two years, the necks of the bottles are placed in an icy-cold brine solution. This freezes the sediment which can then be expelled.

Because the fermentation process has eaten up all of the sugar, the wine is now completely dry and verging on sourness, and therefore it is next given a dose of a bit more sugar. Finally it is corked with special corks that seal it hermetically. The neck of the bottle is then encircled with wire mesh so that the pressure from the gas in the bottle does not blow the cork out. The tops of the bottles are wrapped in gold or silver foil and the wine is finally ready to start working its magic.

There are four major levels of sweetness for Champagne and sparkling wines—*brut*, which is very dry; *sec*, which is dry; *demi-sec*, which is really quite sweet; and the sweet *riche*, which is essentially a dessert wine.

Kosher editions of Champagne as well as sparkling wines from Israel, California and Spain often attain enviable quality.

How to open a bottle of sparkling wine

Champagne and other sparkling wines require special handling because their corks are under a great deal of pressure. If not treated with care, these corks can become dangerous missiles propelled through the air with surprising force. Although the popping of Champagne corks creates a festive atmosphere, it is the wrong way to open a sparkling wine, because in addition to being dangerous, it harms the wine. One of the reasons that Champagne is special is the bubbles, and popping the cork without care reduces the amount of bubbles.

To avoid this, start by peeling off the foil surrounding the cork and neck of the bottle. While applying pressure to hold the cork in, carefully loosen the metal straps holding the cork. After the straps are removed, grasp the cork firmly, continuing to press and gently twist the bottle, not the cork. When you hear the gas begin to escape around the edges of the cork, do not let the cork escape your grip. The gentle hissing sound will be followed by a barely audible pop, this indicating that you have done the job properly. In this way the wine will not form a foam that will suddenly gush out of the bottle, and the bubbles will be preserved.

FRANCE

LOUIS DE SACY, BRUT CHAMPAGNE, GRAND CRU, N.V.: A traditional Champagne, a blend of Pinot Noir, Chardonnay and Pinot Meunier (60%, 35% and 5% respectively). With a good mousse and sharp, long-lasting bubbles, the wine shows deep golden with an orange tint, opens with a rather generous whiff of yeasts, but that settles down quickly to reveal appealing aromas and flavors of red berries, peaches and citrus peel, those complemented by notes of sourdough bread and minerals. Score 90.

LOUIS DE SACY, BRUT CHAMPAGNE, KOSHER EDITION, N.V.: Gold with a distinct orange tint, showing a long mousse and concentrated bubbles that go on and on, showing apple, citrus peel and summer fruits on a lightly yeasty background. Ends with a hint of minerals. Score 89.

NICOLAS FEUILLATTE, BRUT CHAMPAGNE, KOSHER EDITION, N.V.: Crisply dry, with generous minerals on the background and citrus and citrus flower aromas and flavors. Long, complex and delicious, with well-focused bubbles and a long-lasting mousse. Score 91.

HEIDSIECK MONOPOLE, BRUT CHAMPAGNE, BLUE TOP, KOSHER EDITION, N.V.: Categorized as brut but with hints of sweetness. Light-to medium-bodied, with apple, strawberry and yeasty notes. Pleasant but not exceptional and with bubbles that seem unfocused and not quite intense enough. Score 86.

LAURENT PERRIER, BRUT CHAMPAGNE, KOSHER EDITION, N.V.: Rose-petal pink with orange tints. Medium-bodied, with a long mousse and sharp, well-focused bubbles that go on and on, and showing toasty white bread, strawberry, citrus and citrus peel, those backed up by generous hints of spring flowers and minerals. Score 90.

LAURENT PERRIER, BRUT ROSÉ, CHAMPAGNE, KOSHER EDITION, N.V.: Depending on how the light hits, pink towards orange or salmon pink in color, a medium-bodied Champagne, made entirely from Pinot Noir grapes. Light notes of yeast and oak highlight a fascinating array of cherry, red berry, apple and orange peel notes. Fine, long-lasting sharp bubbles, a long mousse and a hint of yeasty white bread that rises on the long finish. Score 91.

POMMERY, BRUT CHAMPAGNE, KOSHER EDITION, N.V.: A traditional blend of Pinot Noir and Chardonnay (55% and 45% respectively). Medium-bodied, with light hints of yeast running through, and a long-lasting mousse. On the nose and palate citrus, apple and floral aromas, those with a light overlay of spiciness. Firm, crisp and long. Score 90.

ISRAEL

GOLAN HEIGHTS WINERY, BLANC DE BLANCS, YARDEN, 2001: The best Blanc de Blancs to date from the winery. Made from Chardonnay grapes by the traditional *methode champenoise*, this medium-bodied sparkling wine shows just the right balance between yeasty sourdough bread, peaches, citrus and minerals. With a generous mousse and sharp, well-focused bubbles that go on and on, this crisp and sophisticated wine goes on to a long, mouth-filling finish. Drink now–2012. Score 92.

GOLAN HEIGHTS WINERY, BLANC DE BLANCS, YARDEN, 2000: A tempting sparkling wine showing appealing summer fruits, citrus and kiwis, those on a background of minerals and just a hint of yeast. A somewhat short mousse but sharp bubbles that linger nicely. Drink now. Score 89.

GOLAN HEIGHTS WINERY, BRUT, GAMLA, N.V.: Made by the *methode champenoise*, a light- to medium-bodied, light golden straw blend of 50% each Pinot Noir and Chardonnay. A generous mousse when poured, sharp, long-lasting bubbles and clean aromas and flavors, opening with citrus and apples and going on to hints of cherries. Good acidity to keep it lively—a good but not overly complex quaffing bubbly. Score 88.

CARMEL, BRUT, PRIVATE COLLECTION, N.V.: A far, far better sparkling wine than Carmel has ever done before. Made by the Charmat method (with the second fermentation accomplished in pressurized stainless steel tanks), a blend of French Colombard, Chardonnay and Viognier (50%, 40% and 10% respectively), with a portion of the Chardonnay oak-aged, shows simple but appealing aromas and flavors of apples, pears and citrus. A short mousse and sharp but not well-focused bubbles here make one think more of Spanish Cava than of French Champagne. Drink now. Score 86.

USA—CALIFORNIA

HAGAFEN, BRUT, NAPA VALLEY, CALIFORNIA, 2001: A blend of 78% Pinot Noir and 22% Chardonnay, a distinctly New World sparkling wine, with a short mousse but concentrated bubbles that go on and on. On the nose and palate tropical fruits, summer fruits and citrus, those matched by notes of chocolate and yeasty white bread. Drink now. Score 89.

SPAIN

ELVI, BRUT, CAVA, N.V.: A blend of Macabeo, Xarel-lo and Parellada grapes, made by the traditional *methode champenoise*. Crispy dry, with concentrated sharp bubbles and appealing cherry, berry and citrus fruits. A pleasant if somewhat light and not complex sparkling wine. Drink now. Score 86.

TIERRA SALVAJE, CAVA BRUT RESERVA, SPAIN, N.V.: Made by the traditional *methode champenoise*, this Spanish blend of Macabeo, Parellada and Chardonnay shows unusually large but sharp and long lasting bubbles. On the nose and palate appealing peach, pineapple and citrus fruits, those backed up nicely by hints of yeasty white bread and minerals. Perhaps a bit more sweet than one might hope for in a wine categorized as "brut," but lively and refreshing. Score 85.

Rosé Wines

For many years rosé wines were perceived as "frivolous"; neither intense nor concentrated enough to be taken seriously by wine aficionados. However, about five years ago, even the most devoted wine lovers began to realize that it was precisely the light, refreshing and even frivolous characters of these wines that gave them great charm, and the popularity of rosé is now on the ascendant.

The best rosé wines are made from the same noble grapes used to make red wines, the difference being that from the time the grapes are crushed they are allowed only very short contact with the skins, that ensuring a lighter colored, less full-bodied, less tannic wine that should be served as well chilled as you would a white. Such wines make excellent warm-weather quaffers and also go well with many lighter dishes, including for example, omelets, grilled fish and chicken or fish salads.

CHILE

TIERRA SALVAJE, ROSÉ, LONTUE VALLEY, CHILE, 2008: Made entirely from Cabernet Sauvignon grapes, somewhere in color between rose-petal pink and peach blush. Light- to medium-bodied, crisply dry with good balancing acidity and appealing cherry, raspberry and cassis fruits. Lively and refreshing. Drink now. Score 87

FRANCE

CHÂTEAU DE GAIROIRD, ROSÉ, CÔTES DE PROVENCE, FRANCE, 2006: A pleasant enough little rosé, rose-petal pink towards orange in color, light on the palate with generous strawberry and raspberry fruits on a gently spicy background and a bare note of sweetness backed up by good acidity. Drink up. Score 85.

BARON EDMOND DE ROTHSCHILD, LE ROSÉ DE CLARK, BORDEAUX, FRANCE, 2008: Made from the free-run juice of Cabernet Sauvignon grapes, fermented entirely in stainless steel, pink towards orange and perhaps more of a "blush" than a true "rosé" wine. Light- to medium-bodied, with just a bare hint of sweetness. Generously fruity with strawberry fruits on a lightly peppery background. Serve well chilled. Drink now. Score 85.

ISRAEL

ASIF WINERY, ROSÉ, ISRAEL, 2008: Dark rose-petal pink, light- to medium-bodied, a crisply dry blend of 95% Syrah and 5% Cabernet Sauvignon showing raspberry, strawberry and cassis aromas and flavors. Lively and refreshing. Drink now. Score 85.

BARKAN WINERY, SHIRAZ ROSÉ, CLASSIC, ISRAEL, 2008: Blush pink, light to medium-bodied, soft, round and lively, with berry, cherry and tutti-frutti notes that make for ideal breakfast or warm-weather quaffing. Drink now. Score 86.

RECANATI WINERY, ROSÉ, ISRAEL, 2008: A light- to medium-bodied blend of Barbera and Merlot (80% and 20% respectively). Cherry red, with aromas and flavors of raspberries, strawberries and red currants, those matched by a light note of what at one moment seems like mint and at another red licorice. Easy and refreshing. Very nice indeed. Score 88.

USA—CALIFORNIA

HAGAFEN, VIN GRIS, ROSÉ, DON ERNESTO, NAPA, 2007: Made entirely from Pinot Noir grapes, showing raspberry, strawberry, red cherry and citrus peel notes, those complemented by notes of nutmeg and cinnamon. Aromatic and not so much crisp as it is soft and round. Drink now. Score 88.

HERZOG, ZIN GRIS, SPECIAL RESERVE, LODI, 2007: Cherry red in color, a dry, lightly oaked rosé showing raspberry, strawberry and cedar notes, those set off nicely by a hint of white pepper. Generous and long for a rosé. Drink now. Score 87.

Dessert Wines

Since the time of the ancient Romans, sweet white wines have been among the most coveted wines in the world. That desirability has never abated, and today kosher wine lovers can enjoy superior sweet wines made in Sauternes, Barsac and the Loire Valley in France, the magnificent ice wines of Germany, Austria and Canada, and the superb Tokaji wines of Hungary. Even several Israeli wineries are producing kosher sweet whites of notably high quality.

The secret of sweet wines, which are often known as dessert wines, lies in their balance, for in addition to flavors reminiscent of apricots, citrus and citrus peel, grapes and honey, these wines, perhaps more than any others, must have fine balancing acidity to keep them from appearing cloying. At their very best such wines are big and luscious, have an intensely rich texture, a flowery bouquet and unmatched elegance, and their delicate sweetness is the result of great expense.

To many, the greatest sweet wines are those made from grapes affected by *botrytis cinerea*. Known as noble rot, botrytis is a fungus that attacks grapes, shrivels them, drains them of water and concentrates their sugar. Because the Israeli climate is not often conducive to botrytis, only one fully botrytized wine was ever made in the country—the 1998 Late Harvest Sauvignon Blanc of the Golan Heights Winery. Since that harvest, not enough grapes have been affected by botrytis to replicate that superb wine, but that has not prevented vintners from isolating small sections of their wineries and there exposing late-harvested grapes to botrytis spores to encourage the development of sweetness. The result, in the Golan Heights Winery's Noble Semillon, has been commendable. At Carmel, winemakers found a small area within one vineyard with grapes impacted by botrytis and then blended those grapes with others to produce a special Single Vineyard wine, the Late Harvest Gewurztraminer of Kerem Shual.

The sweet wines known as *Eiswein* in German and Ice Wine in English were originally made in Germany in the eighteenth century, but now are produced in Canada and New Zealand as well. The process of making those wines involves allowing the grapes to freeze on the vine in temperatures of 7 degrees Celsius (20 degrees Fahrenheit) or below, and then pressing them while they are still frozen. This process leaves the must concentrated and very sweet. In warmer areas, this can be carried on by cryo-extraction, a technique in which the grapes are frozen in the winery. In Israel, for example, the Golan Heights Winery was the first to produce such a wine, Heightswine. That wine was made from Gewurztraminer grapes in their Yarden series in 1998, and has appeared successfully every year since.

In addition to relying on Semillon, Sauvignon Blanc and Gewurztraminer grapes, other kosher dessert wines have relied on late-harvested Muscat and Johannisberg Riesling grapes, and many of those have met with high levels of success, the wines often presenting honeyed, floral and fruity. Another example of a wine that might well be thought of as a dessert wine is the lightly *frizzante* Moscato, from Italy, California and Israel.

Even though most people drink sweet wines primarily with or as desserts, these wines can also serve as excellent aperitifs, as accompaniments to first courses such as goose liver, and to Thai and other spicy dishes, especially those that contain coconut milk. Such wines are also excellent accompaniments to Parmesan, sweet Gorgonzola, well-aged Cheddar and hard or soft goats' milk cheeses. Since the wine should always be sweeter than the dessert with which it is served, it is difficult to match sweet wines with chocolate, but they would be ideal matches to cheesecakes, ripe fruits and fruit-based desserts. Whenever served, these wines are at their best when served chilled to 4–6 degrees Celsius (40–43 degrees Fahrenheit).

Because such wines can be intensely sweet, one rarely drinks them in large quantities and service is often in smaller than usual glasses. Recognizing this, many of the finest dessert wines are bottled in 375 ml. bottles, this allowing a small bottle to comfortably serve six to eight people.

FRANCE—SAUTERNES

CHÂTEAU GUIRAUD, SAUTERNES, 2001: A virtual twin to the non-kosher edition. Deep golden yellow, with a creamy texture and abundant botrytis influence. On the nose and palate honeyed peaches, apples and citrus, matched nicely by generous spiciness. Drink now–2020. Score 95.

CHÂTEAU GUIRAUD, SAUTERNES, 1999: Golden yellow towards bronze in color, full-bodied and with generous apricot, citrus and floral aromas and flavors. Excellent balance between generous honeyed sweetness and natural acidity keep the wine lively. Long and with a hint of ripe melon on the finish. Drink now–2020, perhaps longer. Score 93.

CHÂTEAU PIADA, SAUTERNES, KOSHER EDITION, 2006: Medium- to full-bodied, with a light botrytis influence, generous sweetness and fine balancing acidity. Opens to reveal citrus peel and butterscotch, those yielding to show notes of summer fruit-flavored marzipan. Approachable now, but best from 2011. Score 90.

CHÂTEAU PIADA, SAUTERNES, KOSHER EDITION, 2001: Medium- to full-bodied, with generous botrytis overtones that run throughout and revealing moderately sweet but remarkably rich aromas and flavors of dried summer fruits, citrus peel, and what at one moment feels like white chocolate and another marzipan. Look for a long, honeyed, white-bread finish. Drink now–2012. Score 92.

ISRAEL

CARMEL, GEWURZTRAMINER, LATE HARVEST, SINGLE VINEYARD, SHA'AL VINEYARD, 2008: Generously sweet but with fine balancing acidity, a rich dessert wine, with honey and floral notes to highlight notes of litchi, lemon curd and spices. Complex, long and rich; delicious and complex enough not to accompany dessert but *as* dessert. If you do choose to serve this one with food, please, please, only with fruit tartes or fruit-based mousses. Drink now–2016, perhaps longer. Score 93.

CARMEL, GEWURZTRAMINER, LATE HARVEST, SINGLE VINEYARD, SHA'AL VINEYARD, 2007: Gold, with orange and green tints, medium- to full-bodied, with generous sweetness balanced by lively acidity. Shows litchi, ripe peaches, rose petals, honey and pineapple aromas and flavors, all coming together in a harmonious whole and, on the long finish, notes of freshly baked pecan pie. Drink now–2011. Score 90.

CARMEL, GEWURZTRAMINER, LATE HARVEST, SINGLE VINEYARD, SHA'AL VINEYARD, 2006: Made from grapes harvested in the upper Golan Heights, some affected by botrytis. Moderately sweet, with rose petal and orange peel overtones, and honeyed pear, apricot and litchi fruits. Succulent, with a long-lingering finish. Drink now. Score 90.

DALTON, LATE HARVEST MUSCAT, 2006: Made by the *Solera* method traditionally used in making Port wine. Reinforced with alcohol to a 17% alcohol level, showing clean floral and honeyed notes, those along with fresh and dried apricots and a clear golden color. Clean, sweet, but remarkably refreshing and complex on both the nose and palate. Don't expect to see a release from this wine until at least 2010, but this is one whose development and history I shall follow with great care. Drink now–2015, perhaps longer. Score 90.

ELLA VALLEY VINEYARDS, MUSCAT DESSERT WINE, 2006: Full-bodied with lots of glycerin, avoiding the sometimes too-flowery na-ture of the Muscat grape, and with fine balancing acidity to set off the generous sweetness. Dark gold in color, sitting almost thickly but comfortably on the palate and showing both fresh and dried honeyed apricots, those yielding to pear and raisin compote. Generous and long. Drink now–2011. Score 90.

GOLAN HEIGHTS WINERY, NOBLE SEMILLON, BOTRYTIS, YARDEN, 2004: Golden in color, with fine concentration and balance and developing deep honeyed botrytis-impacted spices and funkiness. On the nose and palate dried apricots, orange peel, toasty oak and tropical fruits that come in towards the long caressing finish. Drink now–2018. Score 92.

GOLAN HEIGHTS WINERY, NOBLE SEMILLON, BOTRYTIS, YARDEN, 2003: Deep and rich, with a concentrated personality of citrus peel, honeyed peaches and botrytis spice. Generously sweet, with fine balancing acidity and a long, sweet and caressing finish on which tropical fruits and butterscotch rise. Drink now–2015. Score 91.

GOLAN HEIGHTS WINERY, HEIGHTSWINE, YARDEN, 2006: This dessert wine is made entirely from Gewurztraminer grapes treated to sub-freezing temperatures at the winery. Showing varietal typicity with litchis, apricots and tropical fruits, all on a spicy background, and showing the floral and honeyed characteristics of an ice wine. Drink now–2012. Score 90.

GOLAN HEIGHTS WINERY, HEIGHTSWINE, YARDEN, 2005: Made entirely from Gewurztraminer grapes frozen at the winery. Pale gold in color, with a complex nose and palate that offers up pineapple, citrus, litchi, orange peel and floral aromas and flavors, those with a light hint of sea water that adds to the wine's charm and complexity. Drink now–2012. Score 91.

KATLAV, CABERNET SAUVIGNON, DESSERT WINE, 2006: Not Port-style, not Madeira- or Sherry-style, a rather unique dessert wine, super-dark garnet in color, full-bodied, with generous but now soft tannins yielding in the glass to generous sweetness, that balanced by natural acidity. On the nose and palate generous ripe plums, berries and cassis, those with overlays of white pepper and chocolate, all leading to a fresh and long finish. A one-off, not to be repeated. Best from 2010. Score 89.

TZORA VINEYARDS, GEWURZTRAMINER, DESSERT WINE, OR, 2006: Light, sweet and silky, almost calling to mind an ice wine, with distinct honeyed pineapple and pear fruits and a hint of kumquat marmalade on the finish. A low 8% alcohol content and good balancing acidity make the wine both lively and tempting. Drink now–2011. Score 89.

USA

HAGAFEN, CHARDONNAY, LATE HARVEST, PRIX RESERVE, NAPA, 2006: Light gold in color, destined to darken nicely with age, full-bodied and generously sweet, a California dessert wine par excellence, with fine notes of botrytis funkiness to complement honeyed apricots as well as poached pears and apples, all coming together very nicely indeed. At its best with fruit-based desserts. Drink now–2016, perhaps longer. Score 92.

AUSTRIA

HAFNER, GRÜNER VELTLINER, EISWEIN, BUR-GENLAND, NEUSIEDLERSEE, 2002: Made in the traditional manner, entirely from Grüner Veltliner grapes that were allowed to freeze on the vine, this concentrating the sugar nicely. Generously sweet, with a good hint of botrytis spiciness and showing fine balancing acidity to keep the wine lively. On the nose and palate an array of dried fruits, including apricots, peaches and apples, those matched by a very appealing peppery overlay. Generous and mouth-filling, good with goose liver appetizers, fruit-based desserts or as dessert. Drink now–2014. Score 90.

HAFNER, SCHEUREBE, TROCKENBEERENAUSLESE, BURGENLAND, NEUSIEDLERSEE, AUSTRIA, 2000: A wine that continues to cross my tasting table and never disappoints. Medium-bodied, moderately sweet with good concentration and fine balancing acidity. Opens to show honeyed peach and apricot fruits on a lightly spicy background. Appropriate as an aperitif or as a dessert wine. Drink now. Score 88.

HUNGARY—TOKAJI

LANGER, TOKAJI, ASZU, 3 PUTTONYOS, 2000: Deep gold in color, showing apricot, orange and tropical fruits. Moderately sweet, with good balancing acidity, and with just enough botrytis spiciness to please. Drink now–2011. Score 88.

LANGER, TOKAJI, ASZU, 5 PUTTONYOS, 1998: Muscular and almost potent in its youth but now, although still intense and concentrated, coming together beautifully. On the nose and palate dried summer fruits and citrus peel together with Oriental spices, those matched by fine acidity to balance the generous sweetness. Long and elegant. Drink now–2012, perhaps longer. Score 91.

LANGER, TOKAJI, SZAMORODI, LATE HARVEST, 1998: Medium-bodied, off-dry with honey and almonds to highlight apple pie aromas and flavors, those supported nicely by notes of vanilla and cinnamon. Look for an appealing spicy finish here. Drink now. Score 87.

LANGER, FURMIT, LATE HARVEST, TOKAJI, 1998: Made entirely from Furmit grapes, with generous botrytis impact showing spicy dried apricots and mandarin oranges. Moderately sweet, with fine balancing acidity, a fine aperitif. Drink now–2011. Score 87.

PORTUGAL

TAYLOR FLADGATE, PORTO CORDOVERO, LBV, 2004: A second joint effort between Royal Wines of the USA and the well-respected Port lodge of Taylor Fladgate. Deep royal purple in color, smooth and rich, medium-bodied and showing moderate sweetness in fine balance with alcohol and currant, plum and  raisin fruits, all supported by spicy, caramel and chocolate notes. Drink now–2018. Score 90.

TAYLOR FLADGATE, PORTO CORDOVERO, FINE RUBY PORT, N.V.: Darker garnet in color than most Ruby Ports and on the palate and nose one might think this a higher-level Tawny. Ripe and spicy, with well-integrated tannins and good balancing acidity, showing generous prune, black cherry, caramel and vanilla along with a firm structure and a generous finish on which you will find a hint of cinnamon. A very well-made Ruby! Drink now. Score 88.

Afterword

Hosting Tasting Parties for Pleasure

Tasting parties hosted for friends or acquaintances can offer the opportunity to taste far more wines in a single evening than is usually possible. At such friendly gatherings, almost always held in a relaxed atmosphere, there is no need to abide by all of the rules set by the professional. There are, however, several guidelines that can make such evenings successful:

- The basic rule in all tastings is that white wines should be tasted before reds, and within each group you should start with wines that are light in body before going on to fuller-bodied wines. When tasting wines of the same varietal, such as Cabernet Sauvignon or Merlot, always start with the youngest wines and end with the most mature.

- Professionals can sample fifty or more wines at a single sitting because they have undergone a rigid apprenticeship and are trained to examine every wine methodically and analytically. It is widely agreed that the maximum number of wines that can be tasted and enjoyed at friendly gatherings at home is eight.

- Wines should be served at their proper temperatures. Young reds should be opened about fifteen or twenty minutes before the tasting, and more mature reds about half an hour before they are poured. In setting up a tasting table, provide enough space so that guests can feel comfortable. Although some people feel that a single glass is adequate for each guest (who will rinse their glasses with water between tastings), I feel that a separate glass should be provided for each wine that is being served. This allows each person to return to earlier tasted wines and compare them to others being tasted, and does not force anyone to rely on memory alone in making comparisons. Be sure that all of the glasses are perfectly clean. Each guest should also be provided with a separate glass for water.

- Wines should be arranged on the table in the order they are to be tasted. I suggest using a marker to put a number on each bottle and then to mark the corresponding number on the base of each glass in order to avoid any confusion.

- After they have tasted each wine, professional wine tasters spit the wine out in order not to become intoxicated. There is no need to spit at a home tasting where much of the pleasure comes from actually drinking the wine. Some guests will choose to spit, however, so there should be enough receptacles on the table for this purpose. (Clay jugs, low vases and Champagne buckets are ideal.)

- At even the most casual of tastings, each of the guests should be given either a pad and pencil or a form that can easily be filled out so that they can record their impressions of each wine tasted. Making notes unconsciously forces people to make up their minds and commit themselves before they reach a general conclusion about the wines being sampled.

- The host or hostess of a wine-tasting has two options—either placing the bottles on the table in full sight of the guests or placing each bottle in a paper bag, each bag identified only by a number, for a blind tasting. My own preference is always for blind tastings, for no matter how honest we may be, the power of suggestion is strong and it is difficult to be entirely objective once one has seen the label of a prestigious Château-bottled wine. Unconsciously or otherwise, advance knowledge often reflects what we think we should find rather than what our senses tell us.

- If the host or hostess of the party is knowledgeable about wine, they should not hesitate to say a few words about each wine being tasted. Under no circumstances, however, should the host or any of the guests present their drinking companions with detailed lectures on the wines. That, frankly, is a bore and contradicts the purpose of such an evening.

- Estimating the number of bottles needed for a tasting is not difficult. Allow half a bottle of all the wines, combined per person. That is to say, for 8 people you will need 4 bottles, for 12 people, 6 bottles. When pouring during the tasting itself, remember that the average sampling should be small enough to allow room for swirling the wine in the glass. Whatever wines are left over after the actual tasting can be served with the meal or snacks offered afterwards.

- Although some disagree, I feel that food should always be served after and never before or during a wine tasting. Although we eventually judge wines partly by how well they go with the foods we like, food changes the taste of wine and a tasting without food allows a different, clearer point of view. If you feel absolutely bound to put something on the table, use only cubes of unsalted and sugar-free white bread.

- Discussing the wines tasted is one of the great pleasures of such evenings. If you choose to host a more formal tasting, discourage your guests from discussing the wines until all have been tasted. This eliminates peer pressure and allows each guest to form his or her own opinion of each of the wines. In a more informal setting, however, free speech can comfortably be the rule of thumb.

- After the formal part of the tasting, it is appropriate to set all of the bottles out so that people can select those they most enjoyed to accompany whatever foods you are going to serve.

How I Do My Wine Tastings

In general, I partake of three kinds of tastings—those I hold in my own home on an almost daily basis; trade and professional tastings that are held by importers or at wine exhibitions; and friendly tastings held at wineries, wine shops, restaurants or at the homes of people kind enough to invite me to share their wines.

Under ideal circumstances tastings are done blind, the taster knowing only the broad category of wines being tasted but not being allowed to see the label. This eliminates biases that might arise from previous experience. This is not difficult to arrange; one person opens and pours the wines into numbered glasses and the taster sees the bottles only after having made notes and assigned scores. The peak time for tastings is during the morning hours, long enough after a first coffee but before one has developed a true sense of hunger. The tasting session actually starts the day before, when a list is compiled of the wines that must be tasted. The next morning, about an hour before the actual tasting, an assistant opens the bottles, adding several wines that are not on the list but which fall into the same category. The purpose of this is to eliminate the possibility of "guessing" at what wines have been set in front of the taster. The wines are then poured in groups of six to eight, each glass being given the same number as is placed on the bottle. Those "flights" are then set on the table. The taster tastes the first flight, makes notes and assigns scores, and then shifts those glasses to the back of the table so that another flight can be set, and this continues until the tasting has been completed. Leaving the glasses on the tables allows the taster to return to the various wines for a retasting to see how the wine has opened over time.

The room in which I do my tasting is well lit and as odor-free as possible; the only things on the table are my notepad, sugar-free and salt-free bread, mineral water, a large sheet of blank white paper, and a bucket for spitting. By the end of the tasting, my notepad contains all of my impressions of the wines and the scores I have awarded them, and only then do I compare the glasses to the bottles, inserting the names of the wines I have tasted.

Many critics instruct their assistants to "double-up" occasional wines—that is to say, to serve the same wine at least twice during a tasting, in glasses with different numbers.

This is an excellent check on the taster's judgment, for if during the course of the tasting the same score or a score of plus or minus one point is awarded, it shows that one was truly focused on the task at hand. On the other hand, scores of the same wine that differ by two or more points indicate that either the taster's palate or sense of concentration was not well-enough honed that morning. In such cases, most critics will simply discard all of the tasting notes from that session and return to those wines on a future occasion.

Several Words about Scores

A great many people walk into wine stores and order this or that wine entirely on the basis of its high score. This is a mistake. A score is nothing more than a critic's attempt to sum up in digits the overall quality of a wine. Scores can provide a valid tool, especially when awarded by experienced critics, but they should not be separated from the tasting notes that precede them; for although a score may be a convenient summary, it says nothing about the style, personality or other important traits of the wine in question and therefore cannot give the consumer a valid basis for choice.

There are, however, three major advantages to scores. First of all, scores can serve as initial guides for the overall impression of the wine in question. Second, scores also give an immediate basis for comparison of that wine to others in its category and to the same wine of the same winery from earlier years. Finally, such scores give valuable hints as to whether the wine in question is available at reasonable value for one's money.

The scores awarded in this book should be taken as merely one part of the overall evaluation of the wine, the most important parts of which are the tasting notes that give details about the body, color, aromas, flavors, length and overall style of the wine. It is also important to keep in mind that scores are not absolute. The score earned by a light and hyper-fruity wine made from Gamay grapes, a wine meant to be consumed in its youth, cannot be compared to that given to a deep, full-bodied wine made from a blend of Cabernet Sauvignon, Merlot and Cabernet Franc, the peak of drinking for which may come only five, ten or even thirty years later on. Numerical comparisons between the wines of the great Châteaux of Bordeaux and those meant to be consumed within weeks or months of the harvest is akin to comparing, by means of a single number, the qualities of a 1998 Rolls Royce and a 1965 Volkswagen Beetle.

Even if there was a perfect system for rating wines (and I do not believe such a system exists), no two critics, no matter how professional or well intentioned they may be, can be expected to use precisely the same criteria for every facet of every wine they evaluate. Even when similar scoring systems are used by different critics, readers should expect to find a certain variation between them. The trick is not in finding the critics with whom you always agree, but those whose tasting notes and scores give you direction in finding the wines that you most enjoy.

My own scoring system is based on a maximum of 100 points interpreted as follows:

95–100	Truly great wines
90–94	Exceptional in every way
86–89	Very good to excellent and highly recommended
80–85	Recommended but without enthusiasm
70–79	Average but at least somewhat faulted
Under 70	Not recommended

Glossary of Wine Terminology

ACIDIC: A wine whose level of acidity is so high that it imparts a sharp feel or sour taste in the mouth.

ACIDITY: An important component of wine. A modicum of acidity adds liveliness to wine, too little makes it flat and dull, and too much imparts a sour taste. The acids most often present in wines are tartaric, malic and lactic acids.

AFTERTASTE: The flavors and aromas left in the mouth after the wine has been swallowed.

AGGRESSIVE: Refers to the strong, assertive character of a young and powerful wine. Aggressive wines are too high in acidity, have harsh tannins, or both, and often lack charm and grace.

ALCOHOL CONTENT: Percent by volume of alcohol in a wine. Table wines usually have between 11.5–13.5% in alcohol content but there is an increasing demand for wines as high as 15–16%.

ALCOHOLIC: A negative term, referring to wines that have too much alcohol and are thus hot and out of balance.

AROMA: Technically, this term applies to the smells that come directly from the grapes, whereas bouquet applies to the smells that come from the winemaking process. In practice, the two terms are used interchangeably.

ASTRINGENT: A puckering sensation imparted to the wine by its tannins. At a moderate level, astringency is a positive trait. When a wine is too astringent it is unpleasant.

ATTACK: The first sensations imparted by a wine.

ATYPICAL: A wine that does not conform to its traditional character or style.

AUSTERE: A wine that lacks fruits or is overly tannic or acidic.

BACKWARD: Describes a wine that is not yet ready to drink, or a wine that has not yet developed its maximum potential.

BALANCED: The term used to describe a wine in which the acids, alcohol, fruits, tannins and influence of the wood in which the wine was aged are in harmony.

BARNYARD: Aromas and flavors that call to mind the barnyard, and when present in excess impart dirty sensations, but when present in moderation can be pleasant.

BARREL: The wood containers used to ferment and hold wine. The wood used in such barrels is most often French or American oak, but other woods can be used as well.

BARREL AGING: The process in which wines mature in barrels after fermentation.

BARRIQUE: French for "barrel," but specifically referring to oak barrels of 225 liter capacity, in which many wines are fermented and/or aged.

BIG: A term used to describe a wine that is powerful in flavor, body or alcohol.

BLANC DE BLANCS: White wines made entirely from white grapes.

BLANC DE NOIRS: White wines made from grapes usually associated with red wines.

BLEND: A wine made from more than one grape variety or from grapes from different vintages. Some of the best wines in the world, including most of the Bordeaux wines, are blends of different grapes selected to complement each other.

BLUSH WINE: A wine that has a pale pink color imparted by very short contact with the skins of red grapes.

BODY: The impression of weight or fullness on the palate. Results from a combination of fruits, alcohol and glycerin. Wines range from light- to full-bodied.

BOTRYTIS CINEREA: Sometimes known as "noble rot," this is one of the few fungi that is welcomed by winemakers, for as it attacks the grapes it shrivels them, drains the water and concentrates the sugar, thus allowing for the making of many of the world's greatest sweet wines.

BOTTLE AGING: The process of allowing wine to mature in its bottle.

BOUQUET: Technically, the aromas that result from the winemaking process, but the term is used interchangeably with aroma.

BRETTANOMYCES: Often referred to simply as Brett, a side effect of yeast that causes a metallic or wet-fur note to develop in a wine. In small amounts Brett can add charm, but in large amounts it is a serious fault.

BRILLIANT: A wine whose color is clear and has no cloudiness.

BROWNING: When a red wine starts to develop a brown edge or a brownish color. Such wines are generally fully mature and will almost surely not improve.

BRUT: Bone dry. A term used almost exclusively to describe sparkling wines.

BUTTERY: A positive term for rich white wines, especially those that have undergone malolactic fermentation.

CARAMELIZED: A wine that has taken on a brown color, and sweet and sour aromas and flavors, often due to exposure to oxygen as the wine ages.

CARBONIC MACERATION: Method of fermenting red wine without crushing the grapes first. Whole clusters of grapes are put in a closed vat together with carbon dioxide, and the fermentation takes place within the grape berries, which then burst.

CHARACTER: Balance, assertiveness, finesse and other positive qualities combine to create character. The term is used only in the positive sense.

CHEWY: Descriptive of the texture, body and intensity of a good red wine. A chewy wine will be mouth-filling and complex.

CLONE: A vine derived by vegetative propagation from cuttings, or buds from a single vine called the mother vine.

CLOSED: A wine that is not showing its potential and is holding back on its flavors and aromas.

CLOYING: A wine that has sticky, heavy or unclean aromas or flavors.

COARSE: A wine that is rough or overly alcoholic. Appropriate in some country-style wines but not in fine wines.

CONCENTRATED: Wines with intense flavors, depth and richness. Synonymous with deep.

CORKED: A wine that has been tainted by TCA (2, 4, 6-Trichloroanisole), increasingly caused by faulty corks. TCA imparts aromas of damp, moldy and decomposing cardboard to a wine. Sometimes only barely detectable, at other times making a wine unapproachable.

COUNTRY-STYLE: A simple wine that is somewhat coarse but not necessarily unpleasant.

CREAMY: A soft, silky texture.

CRISP: A clean wine with good acidity.

CUVEE: A wine selected by a winemaker as special, and separated out for bottling under a special label.

DELICATE: Wines that are valued for their lightness and subtlety.

DENSE: Full in flavor and body.

DEPTH: Refers to complexity and intensity of flavor.

DESSERT WINE: A sweet wine. Often served as an accompaniment to goose liver dishes at the start of a meal.

DIRTY: A wine typified by off aromas or flavors resulting from either poor vinification practices or a faulty bottling process.

DRINKING WINDOW: The predicted period during which a wine will be at its best.

DRY: The absence of sugar or sweetness.

DUMB: A wine that has gone into a dumb period is one that has closed down and is holding back on its aromas and flavors. A natural process in many red wines 12–18 months after bottling.

EARTHY: Clean sensations of freshly turned soil, minerals, damp leaves and mushrooms. Can be a very positive trait.

ELEGANT: A wine showing finesse or style.

EVERYDAY WINES: Inexpensive, readily available and easy-to-drink wines, lacking sophistication, but, at their best, pleasant accompaniments to food.

FAT: A full-bodied wine that is high in alcohol or glycerin but in which the flavor overshadows the acidity, giving it a heavy, sweetish sensation. A negative term.

FERMENTATION: A process by which yeast reacts with sugar in the must, resulting in the creation of alcohol.

FILTRATION: Usually done just prior to bottling, the process of filtering the wine in order to remove large particles of sediment and other impurities. Over-filtration tends to rob wines of their aromas and flavors.

FINESSE: Showing great harmony. Among the best qualities of a good wine.

FINISH: The aromas and flavors that linger on the palate after the wine has been swallowed.

FIRMNESS: The grip of a wine, determined by its tannins and acidity.

FLABBY: The opposite of crisp, often a trait of wines that lack acidity and are thus dull and weak.

FLAT: Synonymous with flabby.

FLINTY: A slightly metallic taste, sometimes found in white wines such as Chardonnays. A positive quality.

FORTIFIED WINE: A wine whose alcoholic strength has been intensified by the addition of spirits.

FORWARD: Can be used in three ways—wines that border on being flamboyant; wines that have matured quickly; or wines that are delicious and well developed.

FRIZZANTE: Lightly sparkling.

GARRIGUE: A wine that hints of scrub brush, Provençal herbs and light earthy notes. A positive term.

GRASSY: A term often used to describe white wines made from Sauvignon Blanc and Gewurztraminer grapes.

GREEN: In the positive sense, wines that are tart and youthful but have the potential to develop. In the negative sense, a wine that is unripe and sour.

HARD: A sense of austerity usually found in young, tannic red wines before they mellow and develop with age.

HARSH: Always a negative term, even more derogatory than "coarse."

HERBACEOUS: Implies aromas and flavors of grass, hay, herbs, leather and tobacco.

HOT: The unpleasant, sometimes burning sensation left on the palate by an overly alcoholic wine.

ICE WINE: A dessert wine made by a special method in which the grapes are left on the vine until frozen and then pressed while still frozen. Only the water in the grape freezes and this can be removed, leaving the must concentrated and very sweet. In warm weather areas the freezing process may be done in the winery.

INTENSE: A strong, concentrated flavor and aroma.

INTERNATIONALIZED WINES: Reds or whites that are blended to please any palate. At their best such wines are pleasant, at their worst simply boring.

LATE HARVEST: In such a harvest, grapes are left on the vines until very late in the harvest season, the purpose being to obtain sweeter grapes that will be used to make dessert wines.

LEES: Sediments that accumulate in the bottom of the barrel or vat as a wine ferments.

LEGS: The "tears" or stream of wine that clings to a glass after the wine has been swirled.

LENGTH: The period of time in which the flavors and aromas of a wine linger after it has been swallowed.

LIGHT: Low in alcohol or body. Also used to describe a wine low in flavor.

LIVELY: Clean and refreshing.

LONG: A wine that offers aromas and flavors that linger for a long time after it has been swallowed.

LONGEVITY: The aging potential of a wine, dependent on balance and structure.

MALOLACTIC FERMENTATION: A second fermentation that can occur naturally or be induced, the purpose of which is to convert harsh malic acid to softer lactic acid.

MATURE: A wine that has reached its peak after developing in the bottle.

MELLOW: A wine that is at or very close to its peak.

METHODE CHAMPENOISE: The classic method for making Champagne by inducing a second fermentation in the bottle.

MID-PALATE: Those aroma and taste sensations felt after the first attack.

MOUSSE: The foam and bubbles of sparkling wines. A good mousse will show long-lasting foam and sharp, small, concentrated bubbles.

MOUTH-FILLING: A rich, concentrated wine that fills the mouth with satisfying flavors.

MUST: The pre-fermentation mixture of grape juice, stem fragments, skins, seeds and pulp, that results from the grape-crushing process.

NOSE: Synonymous with bouquet.

NOUVEAU: Term that originated in Beaujolais to describe very young, fruity and light red wines, often made from Gamay grapes and by the method of carbonic maceration. Such wines are always meant to be consumed very young.

N.V.: A non-vintage wine; a term most often used for sparkling wines or blends of grapes of different vintage years.

OAK: The wood most often used to make the barrels in which wines are fermented or aged. The impact of such barrels is reflected in the level of tannins and in its contribution to flavors of smoke, spices and vanilla to the wines.

OAKED: A wine that has been fermented and/or aged in oak barrels.

OFF: A wine that is spoiled or flawed.

OXIDIZED: A wine that has gone off because it has been exposed to oxygen or to high temperatures.

PEAK: The optimal point of maturity of a given wine.

PERSONALITY: The overall impression made by an individual wine.

RESIDUAL SUGAR: The sugar that remains in a wine after fermentation has been completed.

RICH: A wine with full flavors and aromas.

RIPASSO: A second fermentation that is induced on the lees of a wine made earlier.

ROBUST: Assertive, full-bodied and characteristic of good red wines at a young age, or country-style wines that are pleasingly coarse.

ROTTEN EGGS: Describes the smell of hydrogen sulfide (H_2S). Always an undesirable trait.

ROUND: A wine that has become smooth as its tannins, acids and wood have integrated.

RUSTIC: Synonymous with country-style.

SHARP: Overly acidic.

SHORT: A wine whose aromas and flavors fail to linger or to make an impression after the wine has been swallowed.

SILKY: Synonymous for lush or velvety. Silky wines are never hard or angular on the palate.

SIMPLE: A wine that has no nuances or complexity.

SMOKY: A flavor imparted to a wine from oak casks, most often found in unfiltered wines.

SMOOTH: A wine that sits comfortably on the palate.

SOFT: A wine that is round and fruity, relatively low in acidity and is not aggressive.

SPICY: A wine that imparts a light peppery sensation.

STALE: A wine that has lost its freshness, liveliness or fruitiness.

STEWED: The sensation of cooked, overripe or soggy fruit.

STINGY: A wine that holds back on its aromas or flavors.

SULFITES: Usually sulfur dioxide that is added to wine to prevent oxidation.

SUR LIE: French for "on the lees." A term used to describe the process in which a wine is left in contact with its lees during fermentation and barrel aging.

TANNIC: A wine still marked by firm tannins. In their youth, many red wines tend to be tannic and need time for the tannins to integrate.

TANNINS: Phenolic substances that exist naturally in wines and are extracted from the skins, pips and stalks of the grapes, as well as from development in new oak barrels. Tannins are vital for the longevity of red wines. In young wines, tannins can sometimes be harsh, but if the wine is well balanced they will blend with other substances in the wine over time, making the wine smoother and more approachable as it ages.

TASTED FROM COMPONENTS: A barrel tasting done before the final blend was made.

TCA: 2, 4, 6-Tricholoraniole. See "corked."

TERROIR: The reflection of a vineyard's soil, altitude, micro-climate, prevailing winds, and other natural factors that impact on the quality of the grapes, and consequently on the wines produced from them.

THIN: Lacking in body or fruit.

TOASTING: Searing the inside of barrels with an open flame when making the barrels. Heavy toasting can impart caramel-like flavors to a wine; medium toasting and light toasting can add vanilla, spices or smokiness to the wine, all positive attributes when present in moderation.

VANILLA: Aroma and flavor imparted to wines from the oak barrels in which they age.

VARIETAL TRAITS: The specific colors, aromas and flavors traditionally imparted by a specific grape variety.

VARIETAL WINE: A wine that contains at least 85% of the grape named on the label.

VEGETAL: An often positive term used for a bouquet of rounded wines, in particular those made from Pinot Noir and Chardonnay grapes, whose aromas and flavors often call to mind vegetables rather than fruits.

VINTAGE: (a) Synonymous with harvest; (b) A wine made from grapes of a single harvest. In accordance with EU standards, a vintage wine must contain at least 85% grapes from the noted year.

VOLATILE: A volatile wine has a vinegar-like aroma. A serious fault in a wine.

WATERY: A wine so thin that it feels diluted.

WOOD: Refers either to the wood barrels in which the wine ages or to a specific aroma and flavor imparted by the barrels.

YEAST: A kind of fungus, vital to the process of fermentation.

Index of Wineries

The United States— New York State

Champagne and Sparkling Wines

Rosé Wines

Dessert Wines

About the Author

Daniel Rogov is Israel's most influential and preeminent wine critic. He writes weekly wine and restaurant columns in the respected newspaper *Haaretz*, and contributes regularly to two prestigious international wine books—Hugh Johnson's *Pocket Wine Book* and Tom Stevenson's *Wine Report*. Rogov also maintains a wine and food forum, which can be found at www.tobypress.com/rogov.

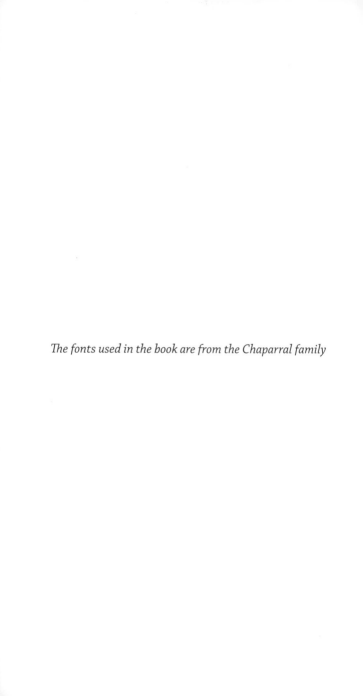

The fonts used in the book are from the Chaparral family

Other works by Daniel Rogov
available from *The* Toby Press

Rogov's Guide to Israeli Wines

Rogues, Writers & Whores:
Dining with the Rich and Infamous

The Toby Press publishes fine writing,
available at bookstores everywhere. For more information,
please contact *The* Toby Press at www.tobypress.com

1. Chateau - France   2001, 2004, 2005
_____

2. Barkan - Superieur — 2005 - 2007

3. Barkan - Reserve

4. Binyamina - Reserve

5. Carmel - Limited Edition
            Single Vineyard
            Appellation

Israel)

6. Domaine de Castel

7. Dalton - Reserve

8. Galil Mountain

7. Yarden - Golan Heights   2003 - 2007
          Series

8. Recanati - Special Reserve
             Reserve

9. Tzora Vineyard

10. Yatir Winery
_____

USA   1. Covenant
       2. Four Gates
       3. Hagafen - Prix Reserve
                 Napa Valley

       4. Herzog